Disclaimer (Exclusive clause)

The author and all employees disclaim any incorrect interpretation, wrong answers to questions or text, harm including emotional, psychological, and physical harm, or any form of liability to the reader/listener or for information given by third parties.
Furthermore, this disclaimer protects all contributors, directors, employees, 3rd parties, authors and will not be liable for any injury caused.

Contents

All Rights Reserved © 1
Disclaimer (Exclusive clause)..1
Preface 6
Dedication..9
Acknowledgement. 9
About the Author..10
I..10
I..11

Chapter 1 13
The Impact of Artificial, Cultural, And Emotional Intelligence on Accounting for Social Responsibility and Sustainability 13
Chapter 2..37
Causes and Consequences of Inflation: Effects on Households, Businesses, Savers, Borrowers, and Government..37
Introduction..38
Understanding Inflation..39
Causes of Inflation..40
Demand-Pull Inflation 40
Cost-Push Inflation 42
Monetary Causes of Inflation..43
Fiscal Policy and Government Deficits..44
Exchange-Rate Depreciation..45
Inflation Expectations 45

Consequences of Inflation 46
Effects on Households..46
Effects on Businesses 48
Effects on Savers 49
Effects on Borrowers 50
Effects on Government..51
F52
Broader Economic Consequences of Inflation 52
Measures for Controlling Inflation 54
Conclusion 56
References 57
Chapter 3 59
THE USE OF SOCIAL MEDIA IN PRODUCT MARKETING IN TABLE 59
Chapter 107
The Use of Social Media in Product Marketing 107
dissertation 107
Literature Review..107
Introduction 107
Social Media and Consumer Communication Techniques 109
Type of Applied Data 111
Chapter 4 114
The Concept of a Firm's Cost Structure 114
Fixed Costs..115
Variable Costs 117

Total Costs 119

Average Costs 120

Marginal Costs 122

Importance of Cost Structure to Business Decisions 125

Business Example: A Manufacturing Firm 126

Conclusion 128

References 129

Chapter 5 130

The Role of Government in a Mixed Economy 130

Meaning and Characteristics of a Mixed Economy 130

Why Governments Intervene in Markets 131

Major Roles of Government in a Mixed Economy 137

Advantages of Government Intervention 141

Disadvantages of Government Intervention 143

Government Intervention and Economic Development 148

The Appropriate Balance Between Government and Markets 149

Chapter 6 150

Artificial Intelligence in Accounting and Auditing – Ethical Use of AI in the Field of Accounting and Auditing 150

Artificial Intelligence in Accounting and Auditing – Ethical Use of AI in the Field of Accounting and Auditing 150

Chapter 7 163

Major Factors That Businesses Should Consider When Expanding into International Markets.........163

Conclusion.........177

References.........179

Author Qualifications.........181

Glossary Economic.........205

Preface

Every business decision is an economic decision. What price should you charge? Should you hire more staff? Should you expand, borrow, or cut costs? Behind every one of those questions is economics. This book, Economics for Business, was written for entrepreneurs, managers, and students who do not need abstract theory. You need practical tools to make better decisions and grow a profitable business. Inside, you will learn: How markets work - Demand, supply, pricing, and competition; costs and profit - Fixed vs variable costs, break-even, and margins; the wider economy - Inflation, interest rates, taxes, and how government policy affects your business; strategy- scarcity, opportunity cost, risk, and making choices with limited resources. I have avoided complicated jargon.

Instead, each chapter uses real business examples to show you how economic principles apply on the shop floor, in the office, and in the boardroom. Economics will help you: Understand your customers better, control your costs, spot opportunities before your competitors, and make decisions with confidence. Business is about solving problems. Economics gives you the framework to solve them well.

Economics is the study of choice. Every day, individuals, businesses, and governments must decide how to use limited resources to meet unlimited needs. This book, Economics, was written to make those choices understandable. Whether you are preparing for A Level, university, or want to understand how the world works.
The aim is to explain core principles clearly, to use real-world examples, and to develop your ability to analyse data, graphs, and policy. Inside you will find: Foundations: Scarcity, demand and supply, markets, and government intervention; Macroeconomics: Inflation, unemployment, growth, and fiscal/monetary policy; Microeconomics: Consumer behaviour, firms, competition, and market failure; Global Economics: Trade, development, and the challenges of the 21st century. Economics is not just about money. It is about people, incentives, and consequences. I hope that after reading this book, you will not only pass your exams but also think more critically about the news, policy, and your own role in the economy.

Why do prices rise? Why do some countries get rich while others stay poor? Why do governments tax, spend, and borrow? This book answers those questions in plain English. Economics affects every part of our lives — from the price of bread to the job market to global trade. However, it is too often taught with too much jargon and too little connection to real life. In these pages I have tried to do the opposite. Each chapter explains one big idea, shows how it works with examples, and explains why it matters to you. Whether you are a student, a business owner, or just curious, this book will give you the tools to understand how economies work and how to make better decisions. The economy belongs to all of us.

Dedication

I dedicate this book to my son Elliot, a Harvard University graduate.

.

Acknowledgement.

As with all the previous one hundred and eighty-one book titles I have written and published, I acknowledge the Guardian's help, knowledge, and wisdom, and the direction Almighty God has given me in writing this book. It would have been impossible to finish writing this book because when I started writing,

I never knew how or when I would end, or where to conduct my research, but once I began, I received more guidance from Almighty God. Without Him, this book would never have been written. He directed and gave me the resources; therefore,

the real author of this publication is God. For example, initially

About the Author

I was an abandoned child at the age of three for another three years when my parents divorced. I spent that time sleeping rough. Slept in the marketplace, railway station and lorry station at Nkawkaw in Ghana. I carried passengers' luggage to feed myself. The dogs in the market were my friends, using my legs for dinner.

I came to the United Kingdom in winter, wearing Oxfam clothes and with ten pounds. Slept on the pavement in Manchester, England, for 7 days before I met my host. During this time, I ate from the rubbish bin and received gifts from passersby.

"From the marketplace to the world stage, from abandoned child to traditional chief—education changed everything. Let us change everything for those who come behind us."

It is pleasurable to see so many people I have helped prosper in life. However, it is painful to see that some family members and one in-law, despite

Economics for Academic and Business. J. Safo my past help, have been ungrateful because I stopped providing funds and advice.

I am the statistical impossibility who became inevitable. I was once abandoned, but now I provide for others. I am the illiterate marketplace boy who now teaches through 195 books in five languages. (Still authoring books on various subjects).

I am the orphan who now fathers movements. I was the homeless child who now holds chieftaincy over one hundred square miles. I started writing books and songs with lyrics to overcome boredom and to be closer to Almighty God—every university claims to transform lives through education. I am living proof. Most institutions' mission statements speak of diversity, social mobility, global citizenship, and lifelong learning—I embody every one of these words. My Master of Laws (LLM) and postgraduate studies in Legal Research and International Law were not academic exercises—they were weapons I forged for justice.

"To facilitate international communication."

Through books in five languages, I communicate across cultures. Through 51 religious texts, I communicate interfaith understanding.

Economics for Academic and Business. J. Safo Through 152 academic books, I communicate knowledge. Through charity, I communicate God's love. Through law, I communicate justice. Through traditional leadership, I communicate the importance of cultural preservation. Through education, I communicate hope. Throughout my life, I have communicated this singular truth: transformation is always possible when faith meets action. When children from African and developing countries see that the abandoned boy became one of the World's most celebrated men, they will believe in their own impossible dreams. When students learn my story, they will understand why giving back is essential. There are three autobiographies, each over 800 pages, that I am currently editing, proofreading, and designing the inside and outside of before I self-publish.

Chapter 1

The Impact of Artificial, Cultural, And Emotional Intelligence on Accounting for Social Responsibility and Sustainability

Accounting and auditing are increasingly dependent on artificial, cultural, and emotional intelligence as stakeholders place greater value on social good, social responsibility, and sustainability. Companies may benefit significantly from information provided by various sources in financial reporting and overall performance. As a result, it is essential to examine how publicly listed firms use this knowledge to advance their corporate social responsibility and environmental sustainability initiatives. By comparing the techniques used by various firms, we can learn more about how artificial, cultural, and emotional intelligence can be used successfully in accounting and auditing. Insights gained from such an analysis may help businesses better integrate diverse information into their operations, thereby increasing their positive impact on society and the environment.

Artificial Intelligence (AI) in Accounting and Auditing

Publicly listed corporations can now integrate corporate social responsibility and sustainability into their business models, thanks to the widespread use of artificial intelligence (AI) in the accounting and auditing profession. To have a positive impact on society, several businesses are using AI to improve their sustainability practices. By analysing massive amounts of data, businesses can better understand their environmental impact, pinpoint inefficiencies, and develop effective plans to reduce waste, energy use, and carbon emissions. Such actions boost productivity, reduce costs, and strengthen a company's image as a responsible citizen. There has been a recent uptick in initiatives that use artificial intelligence (AI) to raise awareness of the importance of sustainable and ethical business practices.

Microsoft is a frontrunner in the IT industry in promoting sustainability, and its use of AI to enhance its sustainability processes is admirable. Artificial intelligence is essential to the company's plan to become carbon neutral by 2030. Microsoft, for one, is using AI to improve energy efficiency in its data

Economics for Academic and Business. J. Safo centres, resulting in substantial savings. In addition to monitoring its supply chain, the firm utilises AI to pinpoint wasteful processes and brainstorm long-term solutions. In addition, Microsoft is harnessing AI to advance circular economy projects by developing recyclable, renewable product designs. These initiatives show Microsoft's dedication to sustainability and provide a compelling case study of how AI may be used to advance more ethical business practices in the IT sector.

Coca-Cola is one corporation using AI to improve its environmental policies and procedures. The corporation has pledged to become carbon- and water-neutral by 2030 and plans to use AI to help achieve that goal. Coca-Cola is taking an essential step in reducing its water impact by using AI to better manage its water use. The corporation also uses AI to lessen its carbon footprint by streamlining its supply chain operations. Coca-Cola is leading corporate environmental responsibility by using AI to improve its sustainability operations. Coca-Cola's efforts are an inspiring illustration of how technology can be used to achieve lofty sustainability goals, and AI's role in supporting sustainable habits is a growing trend.

Retail giant Walmart is among the businesses using AI to further their environmental goals. This firm aims to use only renewable energy by 2035 and is devoted to ethical product sourcing. Consequently, Walmart uses AI to enhance supply chain efficiency and cut carbon emissions to meet this goal. Moreover, one use case is reducing fuel costs by optimising truck routes using AI. In addition to monitoring and analysing energy use trends, the organisation uses AI to identify inefficiencies and develop plans to reduce energy waste. Walmart sets an excellent example for other companies by committing to environmental stewardship and integrating AI into its sustainability programs. This pattern demonstrates how AI can drive substantial improvements in SDG attainment.

Amazon is just one of several corporations using AI to power environmental consciousness. The corporation has committed to becoming carbon neutral by 2040 and is using AI to streamline its supply chain and reduce its carbon footprint. AI-assisted packaging optimisation, for instance, may lead to less garbage and fewer greenhouse gas emissions. In addition, AI is being used to monitor the business's energy use, identify inefficiencies, and develop efficient plans to cut energy waste.

Economics for Academic and Business. J. Safo Amazon is also leveraging AI to improve its logistics operations by optimising delivery routes and lowering fuel use and associated emissions. Amazon is proving its commitment to environmental responsibility and moving closer to realising its objective of supporting sustainable practices across all business operations by embracing AI in its sustainability initiatives.

JPMorgan Chase, a market leader in the financial services industry, is using AI to further its commitment to a sustainable future. The company's goal of facilitating $200 billion in finance for sustainable projects by 2025 is lofty. To do this, the bank is evaluating the sustainability of its loan portfolio and using AI to find sustainable investment possibilities. AI-driven data analysis enables investment decisions that consider environmental, social, and governance (ESG) factors and provides insights to support the company's sustainability initiatives. JPMorgan Chase is using AI to improve its sustainability policies, showing that it is serious about making a positive impact across its business processes and helping make a sustainable future a reality. JPMorgan Chase's initiatives exemplify how technology can be leveraged to achieve sustainability objectives, and AI's application in the

Economics for Academic and Business. J. Safo financial industry is opening up new prospects for sustainable investing.

Artificial intelligence (AI) is used by BlackRock, another major financial services participant, to advance its sustainability goals. The organisation is dedicated to incorporating sustainability into its investment strategies and has set the lofty goal of reaching net-zero carbon emissions by 2050. To help achieve this objective, BlackRock is using AI to assess the climate-related risks of its holdings and identify promising sustainable investing opportunities. Artificial intelligence (AI) helps BlackRock make investment decisions consistent with environmental, social, and governance (ESG) criteria by analysing large volumes of data. The firm is also analysing the environmental impact of its investments and developing plans to reduce carbon emissions using artificial intelligence. BlackRock is using AI to promote a more sustainable future and show its dedication to delivering long-term sustainable wealth for its customers and stakeholders.

Royal Dutch Shell uses Artificial Intelligence (AI) heavily regarding energy sustainability. Intending to achieve net-zero carbon emissions by 2050, the corporation relies heavily on AI to help it achieve that goal. Shell is using AI to improve energy efficiency, reduce carbon emissions, and lessen its negative environmental impact. Using AI, the firm is streamlining its drilling procedures to use less energy and emit fewer greenhouse gases. Shell can now more easily switch to renewable energy thanks to AI-driven discovery and assessment of new sources. Royal Dutch Shell is using AI to improve its sustainability policies, showing its dedication to responsible energy production and paving the way for a greener future.

Therefore, using Artificial Intelligence (AI) to improve sustainability practices and address stakeholder concerns about social responsibility and sustainability is becoming increasingly popular among publicly listed corporations. These businesses are using AI to improve the environmental friendliness of their supply chains, reduce their carbon footprints, and maximise energy efficiency. With the help of AI, businesses can show they care about the environment and earn the confidence of their stakeholders. However, businesses that do not use AI in their sustainability efforts risk falling behind the competition and losing stakeholder support. As a result, using AI to drive sustainable practices is now a critical part of

Economics for Academic and Business. J. Safo corporate social responsibility, and businesses that master this technology will reap long-term advantages for their image, bottom line, and the environment.

Cultural Intelligence (CI) in Accounting and Auditing

Cultural Intelligence (CI) is quickly becoming a sought-after competency among accounting and auditing firms as businesses expand their global footprint and exposure to culturally diverse workplaces. To better understand cultural differences and adapt to local conventions and practices, publicly listed organisations are using CI to establish more inclusive and diverse teams. As a result, businesses can better address local environmental and social issues, improving their corporate social responsibility and sustainability policies. Businesses that use CI can create an environment where everyone feels valued and heard, benefiting the business in many ways. Some concrete ways businesses use CI as a catalyst for CSR initiatives will be discussed below.

Some businesses, including Unilever, use Cultural Intelligence (CI) to improve their eco-friendly procedures. Unilever is dedicated to creating a more

Economics for Academic and Business. J. Safo diverse and inclusive workplace as part of its mission to be a socially responsible and sustainable business. The organisation uses CI to broaden its cultural knowledge and foster an environment where employees from all walks of life feel comfortable and valued. To foster an environment where all workers feel welcome and valued, Unilever has launched various programs to promote cultural diversity and inclusion. Unilever is leading corporate social responsibility and sustainability by leveraging CI to create a more diverse and inclusive workforce.

Intel is just one company using CI to advance corporate responsibility and sustainability. The business is committed to diversity and inclusion and aims to achieve net-positive water use by 2030. Intel is using CI to build a more diverse and inclusive workforce by launching programs to promote cross-cultural competency and appreciation. For instance, the business has launched a global cultural exchange program to foster teamwork and international understanding. In addition, Intel is working to improve water conservation and energy efficiency in its operations, among other corporate social responsibility and environmental sustainability initiatives. Intel is proving its commitment to a more inclusive, egalitarian, and sustainable future for

Economics for Academic and Business. J. Safo everybody by incorporating CI into its sustainability policies.

Retail giant Walmart is among the businesses using CI strategies to improve its environmental impact. The business aspires to achieve zero waste and has launched many programs to raise cross-cultural knowledge and sensitivity. The Global Women's Economic Empowerment Initiative is one such program that targets female employees in Walmart's supply chain. Realising that a varied workforce is essential to achieving its sustainability objectives, Walmart uses CI to build more inclusive and diverse teams. The organisation has also established training sessions to help workers better understand cultural differences and foster an inclusive workplace. To better serve its many communities, Walmart is implementing these initiatives to foster a more sustainable and socially responsible business model. Walmart's use of CI is evidence of its dedication to sustainability and creating an equal future for all people.

Accenture is among the businesses that use CI to strengthen their commitment to corporate social responsibility and environmental sustainability. The company is committed to reducing its carbon footprint through CI and reaching carbon neutrality

Economics for Academic and Business. J. Safo by 2025. Accenture has launched a global cultural awareness training program to foster cross-cultural cooperation, just one of many initiatives aimed at increasing cultural sensitivity and understanding within the company. Developing a diverse and inclusive workforce is crucial to the company's diversity and inclusion strategy, as is ensuring all employees feel respected and appreciated. Accenture's Supplier Inclusion and Diversity Program is an initiative with the same overarching goal: to increase the proportion of diverse and inclusive suppliers within the firm's supply chain. Accenture uses CI to show that it cares about the environment, does good for society, and values its employees by fostering a welcoming and diverse work environment.

Goldman Sachs, a prominent financial services provider, is bolstering its corporate social responsibility and environmental sustainability initiatives through Cultural Intelligence (CI). The organisation is using CI to create more diverse and inclusive teams to reach its aim of facilitating $150 billion in sustainable financing by 2025. Goldman Sachs has created programs to promote cultural awareness and understanding, such as a cultural ambassador program that encourages dialogue and

Economics for Academic and Business. J. Safo cooperation among employees from different cultural backgrounds. The organisation provides training in cultural intelligence to help workers communicate and collaborate more successfully with colleagues from a wide range of cultural backgrounds. Goldman Sachs is committed to creating a more sustainable and fairer future by emphasising sustainability and fostering diversity and inclusion.

Mastercard is one example of a financial services firm using CI to enhance its corporate responsibility and sustainability efforts. Mastercard has committed to achieving zero net greenhouse gas emissions by 2050 and fostering an inclusive and welcoming work environment for all employees. The organisation uses CI to reach this goal by creating a more welcoming workplace for people of all backgrounds. Mastercard has implemented several initiatives to increase cultural sensitivity and tolerance. The Global Cultural Competency Program aims to enhance international understanding and cooperation. The company's goal with these initiatives is to foster an environment where all workers feel valued and respected, regardless of their backgrounds or perspectives. Mastercard and other businesses may boost performance and public perception by incorporating CI into their sustainability plans.

Cultural Intelligence (CI) is being used by General Electric (GE) to improve the company's sustainability efforts in the energy industry. GE plans to employ CI to create more diverse and inclusive teams to achieve its net-zero greenhouse gas emissions objective by 2050. The corporation has a worldwide diversity and inclusion council and other programs to increase employee sensitivity to and knowledge of other cultures. This council aims to increase intergroup understanding and cooperation across cultural boundaries. GE understands that addressing global concerns like climate change requires a culturally inclusive energy industry. GE is enhancing its social responsibility initiatives and establishing an inclusive workplace that promotes diversity and cultural understanding by integrating CI into its sustainability processes.

PwC is another organisation that has shown cultural intelligence in auditing and accounting. Since PwC's clients operate globally, the firm has developed a framework to help them account for cultural differences when preparing financial statements. A client's cultural background can affect

Economics for Academic and Business. J. Safo financial reporting, which is why PwC has developed a framework called "Cultural Awareness for Global Engagement" (CAGE). PwC can work more effectively with clients from various cultural backgrounds and reduce cultural risks by using CAGE. In auditing and accounting, EY has proven itself to be just as culturally astute as PwC. EY values its employees and works hard to attract and retain people from all walks of life, reflecting its commitment to diversity and inclusion. EY has also launched a program called "EY Ripples" to encourage corporate social responsibility and environmental sustainability. Through this program, EY has reduced its carbon footprint, increased its focus on gender equality, and expanded its efforts to support education and entrepreneurship in low-income communities.

Deloitte, an accounting and auditing firm, has demonstrated its cultural intelligence through its team of professionals' commitment to learning about and accommodating customers' diverse cultural backgrounds. This group helps prepare Deloitte employees to engage successfully with clients from diverse cultural backgrounds by providing training and support. The "World-class" initiative is another way Deloitte demonstrates its commitment to

Economics for Academic and Business. J. Safo corporate citizenship. The initiative aims to provide 50 million individuals with education, job training, and economic independence by 2030. Improvements in education, new employment prospects, and long-term economic development are among the goals of this effort, which is being carried out in collaboration with organisations such as the World Economic Forum and the Global Business Coalition for Education. Deloitte is dedicated to creating a more equitable and sustainable world, and its actions in several areas demonstrate that commitment.

KPMG is another major accounting and auditing company that places a premium on cultural awareness. The corporation has recognised the importance of a welcoming and accepting work environment and has launched several initiatives to foster it. One such initiative, "Leading and Learning," encourages people from all walks of life to participate in professional development activities. KPMG also works with groups like the UN Global Compact and the World Business Council for Sustainable Development to spread the word about the importance of ethical business practices. KPMG is leading the way in the accounting and auditing profession toward more diverse, inclusive, and

Economics for Academic and Business. J. Safo responsible practices by emphasising cultural knowledge and keeping the planet in mind.

Therefore, Accounting and auditing organisations need cultural intelligence to succeed in a competitive global market. Still, they must also be sensitive to the cultural ramifications of their actions in the communities where they operate. Accounting and auditing firms heavily influence companies' financial reporting practices, which can have far-reaching effects on local economies and quality of life. Accounting and auditing businesses must appreciate the cultural influence of their work and actively promote ethical and responsible financial practices that benefit local communities in light of the growing importance of social good, social responsibility, and sustainability among their stakeholders.

Emotional Intelligence (EI) in Accounting and Auditing

As businesses have come to recognise the need for a more holistic approach to financial reporting, the role of emotional intelligence (EI) in accounting and auditing has grown. For successful communication and lasting connections, EI's capacity to recognise and control one's emotions

Economics for Academic and Business. J. Safo and those of others is essential. Firms in the accounting and auditing industries need EI capabilities to address the increasing ethical and social challenges they face as stakeholders increasingly prioritise corporate social responsibility, social good, and long-term sustainability. Thus, accounting and auditing businesses must prioritise developing EI capabilities. These capabilities will help businesses face today's problems and earn the confidence of those who matter to them.

Regarding the importance of EI in the accounting and auditing industries, EY sets the bar high. As EY values its customers' satisfaction above all else, it has implemented a program called "Better Starts with You" to help its staff develop emotional intelligence. Staff members may use this program's training and resources to improve their self-awareness, empathy, and communication abilities at work. EY also works with groups such as the United Nations Global Compact and the Global Reporting Initiative to raise awareness of the importance of ethical and sustainable business practices. EY's willingness to address complicated ethical and social concerns is reaffirmed by its collaboration with such groups.

PwC is another exceptional firm in the accounting and auditing sector that exhibits its commitment to EI. PwC has developed a program called "Be Well, Work Well" to encourage workers to improve their emotional intelligence (EI) and better serve their customers. The program's fundamental goal is to improve employees' emotional and mental health at work, which is crucial to developing emotional intelligence. In addition, PwC has set up a Centre for Trust that prioritises earning the confidence of its customers by being transparent and acting in their customers' best interests. PwC's dedication to encouraging a trusting, accountable, and healthy work environment is admirable, and it shows in its emphasis on EI training and the creation of a Centre for Trust.

Deloitte is another accountancy and auditing firm that publicly supports EI. Deloitte has implemented a program called "Unleashing the Power of You" to help its staff develop their emotional intelligence (EI) and better serve its customers. The program provides workers with resources and guidance to help them develop self-awareness, empathy, and communication skills. In addition, Deloitte has developed a " World-Class " program to provide educational opportunities, skill

Economics for Academic and Business. J. Safo enhancement, and employment to 50 million individuals by 2030. By launching this initiative, Deloitte displays its dedication to advancing societal and economic progress and serves as a model for its competitors.

KPMG shares this firm's commitment to developing its employees' EI. KPMG has established a program called "The KPMG Mindset" to cultivate EI among its staff, recognising its importance in building strong customer relationships. Building rapport and trust with clients is a top priority. Thus, the program emphasises introspection, empathy, and clear communication. To further advance responsible business practices, KPMG partners with organisations such as the United Nations Global Compact and the World Business Council for Sustainable Development. KPMG strengthens its reputation as a responsible corporation by cooperating with such groups, demonstrating its dedication to social responsibility and sustainability. KPMG's leadership in the accounting and auditing industry is evident in the firm's commitment to EI development and responsible business practices.

Regarding accounting and auditing, emotional intelligence (EI) is becoming more critical,

Economics for Academic and Business. J. Safo not only at the Big Four accounting firms. Grant Thornton is one such company; it has implemented a "Culture of Belonging" program to encourage employee compassion and acceptance. By empowering workers with EI training and resources, the program hopes to foster an environment that welcomes and values differences among its members. Grant Thornton works with charitable organisations like the American Red Cross and United Way to spread its message of ethical business practices. Grant Thornton is a responsible company because it partners with these groups, demonstrating its dedication to social responsibility and sustainability. Smaller companies like Grant Thornton are making significant gains towards a more sustainable and inclusive future for the accounting and auditing sector by emphasising emotional intelligence and good business practices.

Another company that understands the value of EI in the workplace is BDO, an auditing and accounting firm. BDO Matters is an initiative launched by the firm to promote social responsibility and environmental sustainability across the company's operations. Ethical and appropriate financial procedures, reducing the program's environmental impact, and bolstering community

Economics for Academic and Business. J. Safo economic growth are all priorities. BDO offers staff EI training and resources to foster a compassionate and accepting work environment. BDO is a socially responsible and accountable company, and the "BDO Counts" campaign is one way it shows its dedication to responsible business practices and sustainability. BDO is making substantial strides towards a more sustainable and socially responsible future for the accounting and auditing sector by emphasising emotional intelligence and ethical business practices.

The Big Four accounting firms are not the only ones to see the value of emphasising EI and corporate social responsibility (CSR). T-Mobile US, a mobile phone service provider, illustrates this dramatically. The company's "Team of Experts" initiative designates a group of representatives to work with a single client to improve service quality. As a consequence of this initiative, not only are customers happier, but so are the program's employees. T-Mobile's strategy emphasises the relevance of EI in customer service and relationship development, as well as the social responsibility and ethical behaviours of businesses in the modern world. T-Mobile is more successful as a corporation and has a more beneficial influence on society

Economics for Academic and Business. J. Safo because of this program's emphasis on cultivating a culture of empathy and understanding among employees.

Patagonia, an outdoor clothing manufacturer, has demonstrated a strong commitment to EQ and CSR. Patagonia has developed many initiatives to foster EI in the workplace because it believes it is crucial to developing healthy connections with both consumers and workers. For instance, Patagonia's workers may participate in a mindfulness program that encourages introspection and the cultivation of coping mechanisms. Patagonia's "Tools for Grassroots Activists" program teaches workers to interact better with stakeholders by emphasising empathy and clear communication. Patagonia has attracted top personnel and retained long-time customers because of its commitment to environmental and social responsibility. Patagonia, a pioneer in the outdoor clothing industry and a role model for other firms striving for sustainability and social responsibility, promotes emotional intelligence and social responsibility among its employees.

Microsoft is a firm that places a high priority on workplace diversity and community service. The "Wellbeing" program was established

Economics for Academic and Business. J. Safo because the business recognised the importance of its workers' physical and mental health to its success and sought to address it. Microsoft has also launched a CSR initiative to encourage responsible business practices and environmental preservation. These efforts have enabled the organisation to foster a constructive environment that encourages EI-related traits such as compassion, open-mindedness, and clear communication. In addition, Microsoft has strengthened its image as a socially responsible and ethical business by showing its commitment to social responsibility to its customers and other stakeholders.

Especially in today's environment, when stakeholders increasingly value social good, accountability, and sustainability, emotional intelligence (EI) has become essential to accounting and auditing. A company's image, stakeholder connections, and ability to recruit and retain top talent may all benefit from a focus on EI and social responsibility. Deloitte, PwC, KPMG, T-Mobile US, Patagonia, and Microsoft are just a few examples of industry heavyweights that have demonstrated the value of EI and corporate social responsibility in the workplace. Thus, organisations and their

Economics for Academic and Business. J. Safo stakeholders have several advantages in adopting a socially responsible and emotionally aware strategy.

Conclusion

Ultimately, firms are being held responsible for their social responsibility and sustainability activities, highlighting the significance of artificial, cultural, and emotional intelligence in accounting and auditing. Companies that use this information are better able to make decisions, connect with their constituents, and sustain their operations over time. Companies may boost employee engagement and happiness by creating a more compassionate and understanding work environment through training and support programs that emphasise these abilities. Companies may demonstrate their dedication to social and environmental concerns by partnering with advocacy groups, thereby gaining credibility with their stakeholder base. Businesses that invest in their employees' emotional, cultural, and technological intelligence will be better prepared to face the challenges of today's economy and help create a more just and sustainable world.

Chapter 2

Causes and Consequences of Inflation: Effects on Households, Businesses, Savers, Borrowers, and Government

Causes and Consequences of Inflation: Effects on Households, Businesses, Savers, Borrowers, and Government

Introduction

Inflation is a major macroeconomic issue that affects the cost of living, household purchasing power, business decisions, investment, employment, government finances, and wealth distribution. It refers to a sustained increase in the general price level of goods and services over time, which reduces the purchasing power of money. The International Monetary Fund (IMF) describes inflation as an increase in the cost of a set of goods and services over a period, commonly measured annually (International Monetary Fund [IMF], n.d.). While moderate and stable inflation can coexist with economic growth, high, persistent, or unpredictable inflation can create significant economic and social challenges.

Inflation can result from excessive aggregate demand, rising production costs, supply disruptions, monetary expansion, expansionary fiscal policies, exchange-rate depreciation, inflation expectations, and external shocks such as wars and energy-price increases. Its effects are uneven across economic groups. Households may experience reduced living standards, while businesses face higher costs and uncertainty. Savers can lose purchasing power when returns fall below inflation, whereas borrowers with fixed-rate debt may benefit because inflation reduces the real value of their obligations. Governments may gain through higher tax revenues and reduced real debt values but face increased public expenditure and debt-servicing costs. Therefore, understanding inflation is essential for effective economic decision-making and policy development.

Understanding Inflation

Inflation should be distinguished from an increase in the price of one individual product. If the price of coffee rises because of a temporary shortage of coffee beans, this alone does not necessarily constitute inflation. Inflation involves a broad and sustained increase in the general price level across an economy. Economists commonly measure inflation using price indices such as the Consumer Price Index (CPI), which tracks changes in the prices of a representative basket of goods and services purchased by households. The inflation rate represents the percentage change in the price index over a particular period (Greenlaw et al., 2022). For example, if a household previously required $1,000 to purchase a particular basket of goods and the same basket costs $1,050 one year later, the price level has increased by 5%. If household incomes do not increase by at least the same percentage, real purchasing power declines. Therefore, the effect of inflation depends not only on changes in prices but also on changes in wages, interest rates, taxes, benefits, and asset values.

Inflation can occur at different rates. Low and stable inflation may have relatively limited effects on economic activity. However, high inflation can make it difficult for households and businesses to plan because future prices become uncertain. Very high inflation, or hyperinflation, can severely undermine confidence in a country's currency and financial system (Greenlaw et al., 2022). OpenStax notes that persistent high inflation can distort price signals, complicate savings and investment decisions, and interfere with efficient economic decision-making.

Causes of Inflation

Demand-Pull Inflation

One major cause of inflation is demand-pull inflation. This occurs when aggregate demand for goods and services outpaces the economy's ability to produce them. Aggregate demand includes household consumption, business investment, government expenditure, and net exports. When consumers have more disposable income, businesses increase investment, government spending expands, or exports rise significantly, total demand may increase.

If production cannot increase sufficiently to meet this additional demand, businesses respond by raising prices. For example, if consumers suddenly have more money to spend but the supply of food, housing, transportation, and other goods remains relatively fixed, sellers may increase prices because buyers are competing for limited supplies. According to Greenlaw et al. (2017), this situation can be summarised as “too much money chasing too few goods”

Demand-pull inflation may occur during periods of rapid economic expansion. Expansionary monetary policy can increase aggregate demand by lowering interest rates, thereby encouraging borrowing, investment, and consumption. Similarly, expansionary fiscal policy, such as increased government spending or tax reductions, can increase aggregate demand. Research by Cevik and Miryugin (2025) indicates that expansionary fiscal policy can contribute to higher inflation,

Economics for Academic and Business. J. Safo demonstrating the relationship between fiscal conditions and price pressures.

Cost-Push Inflation

Cost-push inflation occurs when the cost of producing goods and services increases. Businesses face costs for labour, raw materials, energy, transportation, rent, technology, and financial capital. When these costs rise significantly, firms may raise product prices to maintain profitability. Energy prices are particularly important because fuel and electricity are inputs into almost every part of an economy. An increase in oil prices, for example, raises transportation and production costs. Farmers may face higher costs for fuel and fertilisers, manufacturers may pay more for electricity and raw materials, and retailers may incur higher transportation expenses. These increased costs can eventually be passed on to consumers.

Supply-chain disruptions can also produce cost-push inflation. Shortages of essential components, transportation bottlenecks, labour shortages, or international trade disruptions can reduce the supply of goods while demand remains unchanged. When supply falls below demand, prices may increase. Such supply shocks were particularly important during periods of global disruption following the COVID-19 pandemic.

Monetary Causes of Inflation

Monetary conditions can also contribute to inflation. When the supply of money and credit grows substantially faster than the economy's production of goods and services, aggregate demand may increase. If this process continues, it can place upward pressure on prices.
Extreme monetary expansion can produce particularly severe inflation. Historical experience shows that governments that finance persistent, large fiscal deficits through money creation can generate very high inflation. OpenStax explains that extreme cases of government financing through money creation can result in hyperinflation. This results in increasing amounts of money chasing insufficient quantities of goods and services (Greenlaw et al., 2022).

However, monetary expansion does not automatically result in inflation in every circumstance. The relationship depends on economic conditions, the velocity of money, expectations, production capacity, and the behaviour of households and firms. Therefore, inflation should be understood through the interaction of monetary, fiscal, demand, supply, and institutional factors.

Fiscal Policy and Government Deficits

Government fiscal policy can influence inflation through taxation and public expenditure. When governments increase spending significantly without corresponding increases in taxation or productive capacity, aggregate demand may rise. If the economy is already operating near capacity, additional government demand may contribute to inflation.

Cevik and Miryugin (2023), using international evidence covering numerous countries, found that expansionary fiscal policy shocks can increase both headline and core inflation. This suggests that fiscal policy is an important factor in understanding inflation, particularly when governments pursue substantial fiscal expansion during periods of strong demand. Large fiscal deficits may become especially problematic when governments have limited access to borrowing and resort to monetary financing. Such situations can weaken confidence in the currency and increase inflationary expectations.

Exchange-Rate Depreciation

A country's exchange rate can also affect inflation. When the domestic currency loses value relative to foreign currencies, imported products become more expensive. This is particularly important for countries that rely heavily on imported fuel, food, machinery, medicine, or industrial inputs.

For example, if a country imports petroleum in U.S. dollars and its domestic currency depreciates significantly against the dollar, the domestic cost of fuel may increase even if the international price of petroleum remains unchanged. Higher fuel costs then increase transportation and production costs throughout the economy, contributing to broader inflation.

Exchange-rate depreciation can therefore create imported inflation. The effect tends to be stronger in economies with high dependence on imports and limited domestic production capacity.

Inflation Expectations

Inflation can also become self-reinforcing through expectations. If workers expect prices to increase rapidly, they may demand higher wages to protect their purchasing power. Businesses facing higher labour costs may increase prices. Consumers who expect future prices to be higher may accelerate purchases, increasing current demand. Businesses may also raise prices in anticipation of higher future costs.

This process can create an inflationary cycle involving prices, wages, and expectations. If inflation expectations become deeply established, reducing inflation may require stronger monetary and fiscal policies. Maintaining confidence in monetary institutions is therefore important for preventing temporary price increases from becoming persistent inflation.

Consequences of Inflation

Inflation has several economic and social consequences. Its effects depend on its magnitude, duration, predictability, and whether incomes and contracts adjust to price changes.

Effects on Households

Households are among the groups most directly affected by inflation because they purchase goods and services every day. When food, housing, transportation, electricity, education, healthcare, and other essential items become more expensive, household purchasing power declines if income does not rise at the same rate.

For low-income households, inflation can be especially damaging because a larger proportion of their income is generally devoted to necessities. Families may respond by reducing spending on non-essential goods, purchasing cheaper substitutes, delaying major purchases, or reducing savings. High food and energy inflation can therefore have a particularly severe effect on household welfare.

Inflation can also reduce real wages. A worker receiving a 5% nominal wage increase when inflation is 8% has experienced a decline in real purchasing power of approximately 3%, assuming other factors remain constant. Thus, nominal wage growth does not necessarily mean that workers are economically better off.

Inflation can also increase inequality because households have different sources of income and different types of assets. Individuals with fixed pensions or fixed salaries may be more vulnerable than individuals whose wages adjust rapidly. Similarly, households that own property or other inflation-sensitive assets may be better positioned than those whose wealth is primarily held in cash.

The IMF (2023) emphasises that the distributive effects of inflation are complex and that vulnerable households can experience significant welfare losses during periods of high inflation. Consequently, inflation is not simply a macroeconomic statistic; it directly influences living standards and social welfare.

Effects on Businesses

Inflation has mixed consequences for businesses. On the negative side, firms face rising costs for labour, raw materials, energy, transportation, rent, and finance. When businesses cannot pass these increased costs to consumers, their profit margins decline. Inflation also creates uncertainty. Businesses must make decisions concerning investment, production, pricing, wages, inventory, and borrowing. When future costs and revenues are difficult to predict, firms may postpone long-term investment.

OpenStax notes that persistent inflation can cause businesses and individuals to devote resources to protecting themselves against inflation instead of focusing on productive economic activities (Greenlaw et al., 2022). However, inflation can increase nominal revenues for businesses when firms can raise prices. A business that sells products at higher prices may report increased nominal sales even if its real output has not changed. Businesses with strong market power may be better able to pass cost increases to consumers. Inflation also affects labour markets. Workers may demand higher wages to maintain their purchasing power, increasing labour costs for businesses. Firms may respond by raising prices, reducing hiring, improving productivity, or substituting technology for labour.

Effects on Savers

Inflation can be particularly harmful to savers when the nominal return on savings is below the inflation rate. The real interest rate can be approximated as the nominal interest rate minus the inflation rate. For example, if a savings account pays 4% interest while inflation is 7%, the saver earns a negative real return of approximately 3%. This means that although the amount of money in the savings account increases in nominal terms, its purchasing power decreases. A person may therefore have more money in the account but be able to purchase fewer goods and services with it.

Inflation can be especially problematic for people saving for retirement. Long-term savings plans depend heavily on the real return on investments. If inflation remains high for many years, the amount needed to achieve a particular retirement standard of living increases.

However, the impact on savers depends on the type of assets held. Individuals who invest in assets whose values or returns adjust with inflation may be better protected than those who hold large amounts of cash or fixed-interest investments.

Effects on Borrowers

Inflation can benefit borrowers who have fixed-rate nominal debt. This occurs because inflation reduces the real value of money used to repay the debt. Suppose an individual borrows $100,000 at a fixed interest rate. If prices and wages rise substantially over time, the borrower may repay the loan using money that has less purchasing power than the money originally borrowed. Therefore, unexpected inflation can transfer wealth from lenders to borrowers. Doepke and Schneider (2006) describe unexpected inflation as a redistribution shock that reduces the real value of nominal claims and transfers wealth from lenders to borrowers. Businesses with substantial fixed-rate debt may similarly benefit because their liabilities become smaller in real terms. Historical evidence also shows that inflation can reduce real debt burdens for firms with nominal liabilities (Brunnermeier et al., 2025).

However, borrowers are not always beneficiaries. When inflation becomes high, lenders and financial institutions typically demand higher interest rates to compensate for the expected loss of purchasing power. New borrowers may consequently face more expensive loans. Individuals with variable-rate loans may also experience increased repayment costs when interest rates rise in response to inflation.

Effects on Government

Inflation has complex consequences for governments. One potential benefit is that inflation can reduce the real value of existing government debt denominated in nominal terms. If a government borrowed money at a fixed nominal interest rate, inflation reduces the purchasing power of the money used to repay that debt. Inflation can also increase government tax revenues because many taxes are based on nominal incomes, sales, and profits. As prices and wages rise, tax collections may increase even if real economic activity has not increased proportionately.

However, governments also face high costs. Public-sector wages, pensions, healthcare expenditure, infrastructure costs, and social assistance programs may become more expensive.

If government benefits are indexed to inflation, public expenditure rises automatically. Even when benefits are not indexed, governments may face political pressure to increase assistance to households affected by rising prices.

Inflation can also increase government borrowing costs. Central banks commonly respond to persistent inflation by raising policy interest rates. Higher interest rates can increase the cost of issuing new government debt and refinancing existing debt. As a result, governments may have to allocate a larger proportion of their budgets to debt servicing. Fiscal policy can therefore play an important role in inflation stabilisation. The IMF (2023) argues that well-designed fiscal policy can support price stability while protecting vulnerable groups. Governments must balance the need to support households with the risk that excessive fiscal stimulus will increase aggregate demand and worsen inflation.

Broader Economic Consequences of Inflation

Beyond its effects on particular groups, inflation can influence the entire economy. One important consequence is reduced purchasing power. Another is uncertainty. When inflation is unpredictable, households and businesses have difficulty determining the future real value of money, wages, profits, investments, and debts. Inflation can also distort price signals. Prices normally communicate information about scarcity and demand. If all prices are increasing rapidly, it becomes more difficult to determine whether the price of a particular product has increased because it has become relatively scarce or simply because the general price level has increased.

Another consequence is reduced long-term investment. Businesses may hesitate to commit capital to projects when future input costs, interest rates, and consumer demand are uncertain. This can reduce productivity growth and potentially lower long-term economic growth. Inflation may also redistribute wealth. Unexpected inflation generally disadvantages people holding fixed nominal assets and benefits people with fixed nominal liabilities. The redistribution is not necessarily equal across society because households differ in their assets, debts, income sources, and consumption patterns. Auclert (2019) demonstrates that monetary policy and unexpected inflation can have important redistributive effects because households differ in their exposures to income, interest rates, and nominal assets.

At very high levels, inflation can undermine confidence in the currency. People may attempt to spend money rapidly before it loses further value, which can increase the velocity of money and worsen inflation. In extreme cases, individuals and businesses may move toward foreign currencies or barter systems. Hyperinflation can therefore damage the basic functioning of an economy.

Measures for Controlling Inflation

Governments and central banks use several strategies to control inflation. Monetary policy is one of the most important. Central banks can increase interest rates to make borrowing more expensive and savings more attractive. Higher interest rates generally reduce consumption and investment, thereby lowering aggregate demand.

Central banks can also use other monetary tools to restrict liquidity and credit. The objective is to bring demand into better balance with productive capacity while maintaining confidence in the currency.

Fiscal policy can complement monetary policy. Governments can reduce unnecessary expenditure, increase taxes where appropriate, or postpone non-essential spending during periods of excessive demand. However, fiscal tightening must be carefully designed because excessive reductions in government spending can harm employment and economic growth.

Supply-side policies can also address inflation. Governments can invest in infrastructure, energy production, agricultural productivity, transportation systems, education, and technology to increase productive capacity. Improving supply can reduce cost pressures and make the economy more resilient to shocks.

Indexation can protect some households from inflation by automatically adjusting wages, pensions, or other payments according to changes in the price level. However, extensive indexation can also contribute to inflation persistence if wages and prices continually adjust upward. Greenlaw et al. (2017) note that indexing can reduce some of the redistributive effects of inflation but does not eliminate the underlying causes.

Finally, governments need credible economic institutions. Independent and credible central banks, responsible fiscal management, sound financial systems, and clear communication can help stabilise inflation expectations. Maintaining confidence is particularly important because expectations can influence wage-setting, pricing, saving, and investment decisions.

Conclusion

In summary, inflation is a sustained increase in the general price level that reduces the purchasing power of money. It can result from demand-pull pressures, rising production costs, supply disruptions, monetary expansion, expansionary fiscal policy, exchange-rate depreciation, and inflation expectations. These factors often operate simultaneously. Although moderate inflation may coexist with economic growth, persistent and unpredictable inflation can create high economic and social costs.

Inflation affects economic groups differently. Households face higher living costs and see their real incomes decline when wages fail to keep pace with prices. Businesses experience higher production costs and greater uncertainty but may raise prices to protect revenue. Savers may lose purchasing power when returns are below inflation, while borrowers with fixed-rate debt can benefit because inflation reduces the real value of their obligations. Governments may benefit from reduced real debt and higher nominal tax revenues but face increased expenditure and borrowing costs. Overall, high inflation creates uncertainty, distorts economic decisions, and can weaken investment and growth.

Economics for Academic and Business. J. Safo
Effective monetary and fiscal policies are therefore essential for maintaining price stability.

References

Auclert, A. (2019). Monetary policy and the redistribution channel. *American Economic Review, 109*(6), 2333–2367. https://doi.org/10.1257/aer.20160137

Brunnermeier, M., Correia, S., Luck, S., Verner, E., & Zimmermann, T. (2025). The debt-inflation channel of German (Hyper) inflation. *American Economic Review*, *115*(7), 2111–2150. https://www.aeaweb.org/articles?id=10.1257/aer.20230685

Cevik, S., & Miryugin, F. (2025). It is never different: Fiscal policy shocks and inflation. *Comparative Economic Studies*, *67*(1), 186–220. https://ideas.repec.org/a/pal/compes/v67y2025i1d10.1057_s41294-024-00238-w.html

Greenlaw, S. A., Shapiro, D., & MacDonald, D. (2022). *Principles of economics 3e*. OpenStax. https://openstax.org/details/books/principles-economics-3e

International Monetary Fund. (2023, April 3). *Fiscal policy can help tame inflation and protect the most vulnerable*. https://www.imf.org/en/blogs/articles/2023/04/03/fisc

Economics for Academic and Business. J. Safo
al-policy-can-help-tame-inflation-and-protect-the-most-vulnerable

International Monetary Fund. (n.d.). *Inflation: Prices on the rise.* https://www.imf.org/en/publications/fandd/issues/series/back-to-basics/inflation

Doepke, M., & Schneider, M. (2006). Inflation as a redistribution shock: Effects on aggregates and welfare. https://ideas.repec.org/p/cpr/ceprdp/5939.html

Greenlaw, S. A., Shapiro, D., Richardson, C., Sonenshine, R., Keenan, D., MacDonald, D., ... & Moledina, A. (2017). *Principles of Microeconomics 2e. for AP® Courses*. Rice University. https://openstax.org/books/principles-microeconomics-2e/pages/preface

Chapter 3

THE USE OF SOCIAL MEDIA IN PRODUCT MARKETING IN TABLE

SOURCE	How You Found It	Key Theme	Importance of Source to the Topic
, M., & Verma, D. (2020, April 14). *A critical review of digital marketing*. SSRN. Retrieved April 9, 2023, from https://papers.ssrn.com/sol3/papers.cfm?abstract_id=3545505	The article was found through Google Scholar.	Presents a description of the current trends in marketing. For example, it discusses the cost impact of using digital marketing within a business.	The paper provides extensive information on current and future activities in the field of marketing. It supports the topic by presenting contemporary

			practices within the business world. There is an in-depth analysis of concepts like SEO, SEM, influencer marketing, content marketing, e-commerce marketing, and social media marketing. Compani

			es use different digital marketing channels to demonstrate the target markets they intend to reach.
azzi, R. (2015). *Social Media Marketing in Tourism and Hospitality*. SpringerLink. Retrieved April 9, 2023, from https://link.springer.com/book/10.1007/9	The book was obtained from the Springer database.	The author examines the different social media programs handled within the tourism and hospitality sector. The book further highlights the impact of	The book is essential to the topic, as it addresses both theoretical and practical issues and

78-3-319-05182-6		demand and supply issues within the industry.	discusses real-world business experiences in the sector. The information is further split into three sections: recent trends in social media, the impact of social media on traveller behaviour, and future trends

			within mobile marketing technolog ies.
Tuten, T. L. (2008). *Advertising 2.0: Social Media Marketing in a Web 2.0 world*. Praeger Publishers.	The book was obtained from the ABC-CLIO online library	The book looks into the impact of social media marketing on businesses. The author also looks into the social influence on consumer product reviews.	The book is essential to the topic, as it covers business es' different approach es to marketing their products. A company' s additional media platforms attract a

			particular population, indirectly impacting the business's growth. Marketing techniques also affect customers, shifting the types of customers visiting the company. It will also help in understanding the impact of developin

			g a brand through social media.
el, G., Grewal, L., Hadi, R., & Stephen, A. T. (2019). The future of social media in marketing. *Journal of the Academy of Marketing Science*, *48*(1), 79–95. https://doi.org/10.1007/s11747-019-00695-1	The article was obtained from SpringerLink. The report is in the Academy of Marketing Science Journal.	The author focuses on the future of social media in marketing. The author applies themes of the immediate, near, and far ends.	The content is essential to the topic as it illustrates companies' customer engagement patterns. It is important to note how social media platforms affect people and

			businesses. This content offers an analogy for where marketing practices are headed. The different themes help discuss the predictions and identify the relevant future directions for handling

			marketing practices.
ucksman, M. (2017). *The rise of social media influencer marketing on lifestyle branding: A* ... Retrieved April 9, 2023, from https://www.media-education-portal.com/uploads/1/2/4/7/124735657/08_lifestyle_branding_glucksman.pdf	The content is borrowed from Elon University. It is a thesis submitted in partial fulfilment of the requirements of an undergraduate course in communications.	The thesis looks at the rise of social media influencer marketing in lifestyle branding. The author did a qualitative analysis of posts by social media influencers.	The content is helpful for the topic, as it offers in-depth coverage of marketing to individuals and the market. The paper helps illustrate the concept of consumer behaviour when a

			company uses people of interest in its target markets. Many advance ments in the marketing field also impact business operation s within the company' s marketing practices.
lason, A. N., Narcum, J., & Mason, K. (2021). Social media	The article was obtained from Taylor &	The report examines how social media marketing	The article is essential to the topic as it

marketing gained importance after COVID-19. *Cogent Business & Management*, *8*(1). https://doi.org/10.1080/23311975.2020.1870797	Francis Online	practices have gained importance after the global pandemic. It examines customers' unique approaches to social media use in the United States. The paper utilised a consumer Decision-Making Model to investigate changes in consumer behaviour when deciding	discusses customer behaviour during and after a pandemic. There is a significant change in markets during a crisis, affecting global business. The article shows how new ideologies are applied in industry

		which product to use.	in the event of an emergency on the worldwide market.
illai, C., Terho, H., Cardinali, S., & Pascucci, F. (2019). Advancing Social Media Driven Sales Research: Establishing conceptual foundations for B-to-B social selling. *Industrial Marketing Management*, *82*, 293–308. https://doi.org	The article was borrowed from the ScienceDirect database.	The article examines business markets and the changes triggered by increased digitisation. Practitioners and academics have also started emphasising the concept of social selling and a new approach to	The article will help gather information on the roles of the sales team in contemporary business markets. The article also offers information on

/10.1016/j.indmarman.2019.01.002		addressing emerging opportunities and challenges at the sales-force level. The authors further comment that an extended research program on social media usage is needed to understand social selling as a significant application of digital marketing principles at the individual	marketing theory and practice.

		salesperson level.	
., Larimo, J., & Leonidou, L. C. (2020). Social media marketing strategy: Definition, conceptualisation, taxonomy, validation, and future agenda. *Journal of the Academy of Marketing Science*, *49*(1), 51–70. https://doi.org/10.1007/s11747-020-00733-3	The article was obtained from SpringerLink. The article is in the Academy of Marketing Science Journal.	The article examines the growing recognition of social media among companies. There is a research gap regarding the concept of SMMS. The authors propose a taxonomy classifying the SMMAs into four types based on their strategic maturity levels. These SMMSs are	The article is helpful to the topic as it discusses social media marketing strategy. The paper combines the different trends in the proposed media strategy within the business.

		validated using information from previous empirical studies. The article also provides fruitful directions for future research based on input from scholars specialising in this field.	
, S., Mulcahy, R., & Parkinson, J. (2020). When less is more: The impact of Macro and Micro Social Media	The article was borrowed from Taylor & Francis Online.	The article discusses the effectiveness of endorsing products through social media influencers. The article	The article is essential to the topic, as it outlines the outcomes of using

influencers' disclosure. *Journal of Marketing Management*, *36*(3-4), 248–278. https://doi.org/10.1080/0267257x.2020.1718740		also examines various policies and regulations governing business transactions with social media influencers. There are strong links between high and low levels of disclosure of native advertising sponsorships and clients' product evaluations. The article further demonstrates	micro- or macro-level social media influencers in business. It is also helpful as it discusses theory, practice, and policy concepts.

		that a two-by-two experiment indicates that clients exposed to a micro-influencer condition exhibit high levels of product knowledge.	
senberry, K. A. (2021). *Social Media Strategy: Marketing, advertising, and public relations in the consumer revolution*. Rowman & Littlefield.	The book is borrowed from the Rowman & Littlefield library	The book examines social media strategy, focusing on marketing, advertising, and public relations practices. These concepts have an	The book is significan t to the topic, illustratin g the scale and scope of social media for a business.

		indirect impact on business development.	Managers apply different approaches in handling business programs. Additional factors are considered when evaluating the decline of Push Marketing. There are many benefits associated with social media

			strategy. Additionally, the book provides information on social media law, ethics, and etiquette.
ewal, D. *et al.* (2019). "The Future of Technology and Marketing: A Multidisciplinary Perspective," *Journal of the Academy of Marketing Science*,	The article was borrowed from SpringerLink. The article is in the Academy of Marketing Science Journal.	The authors examine the future of technology and marketing. New technologies are believed to have created a stir in every aspect of	The article is essential to the topic as it delivers the impact of new technology on marketing practices.

48(1), pp. 1–8. Available at: https://doi.org/10.1007/s11747-019-00711-4.		human development, including how companies market their products and services. The internet, greater computing capacity, and mobile devices significantly impact business development programs. Similarly, the article integrates the concepts of AI, IoT, and robotics and examines their impact	Managers use various technological approaches to raise awareness of the products being traded.

		on marketing practices.	
rchers, N. S. (2021). *Social Media Influencers in strategic communication.* Routledge.	The book was borrowed from the Taylor & Francis Online Library.	The book provides insight into research on the strategic use of social media influencers within a business. The search database included an estimated 154 peer-reviewed publications about influencer marketing approaches. The details included records from	This is an essential book for research, as it provides insights into recent trends in marketing activities. Multiple changes are recorded in marketing, requiring further research to identify

		2018-2020. These recent reports help to understand marketing trends and enable projections on what may happen in the marketing business in the forthcoming years.	future practices.
Bashir, N., Papamichail, K. N., & Malik, K. (2017). Use social media applications to support new product development processes in	The article was borrowed from the ScienceDirect database.	The article examines the ideologies underpinning the use of social media in new product development processes. The authors	The article is important to my topic because its results further suggest that social

multinational corporations. *Technological Forecasting and Social Change*, *120*, 176–183. https://doi.org/10.1016/j.techfore.2017.02.028		rely on an in-depth analysis of MNCs globally, reflecting on fast-moving consumer goods. A significant amount of money is generated from consumer goods, which then calls for unique marketing techniques to persuade clients to make these purchases. Obtaining an in-depth	media can be clustered as an informal source for understanding a client's preferences, competitors' business approaches, market trends, and product feedback.

		analysis will require qualitative approaches in data collection and analysis.	
Bhimani, H., Mention, A.-L., & Barlatier, P.-J. (2019). Social Media and Innovation: A systematic literature review and future research directions. *Technological Forecasting and Social Change*, *144*, 251–269.	The article was borrowed from the ScienceDirect database	The article examines the relationship between social media and innovation. Future practices are intended to improve media advertising techniques applied in society. Social media is, however, seen as the	The article is essential to the topic, as it shows different techniques that will help improve marketing practices with the clientele.

https://doi.org/10.1016/j.techfore.2018.10.007		vehicle for generating rich data with unique multi-faceted insights to drive quick ideation and commercialisation of client innovations	
ıstantinides, E. (2014). Foundations of social media marketing. *Procedia - Social and Behavioural Sciences*, *148*, 40–57. https://doi.org/10.1016/j.sbspro.2014.07.016	The article was borrowed from the ScienceDirect database	The article illustrates how social media has altered power structures within the marketplace. It further demonstrates that these changes have created a new breed of powerful,	The article's importance to the topic is evident in its recognition of media as a major driver of change among society's

		complex customers who are hard to influence or persuade. Social media has become a customer empowermen t agent	current clientele.
ı, U., & Alatas, B. (2019). A new direction in social network analysis: Online Social Network Analysis Problems and applications. *Physica A: Statistical Mechanics and Its*	The article was borrowed from the ScienceDir ect database	The article examines the progress made by social media networks in recent years, taking into account factors such as global reliance on the internet. Reaching social networking	The article is essential to the topic, as it outlines the milestone s the internet has brought to advertisin g practices.

Applications, *535*, 122372. https://doi.org/10.1016/j.physa.2019.122372		platforms like Twitter, Instagram, Facebook, and LinkedIn is now easier.	
Ali Taha, V., Pencarelli, T., Škerháková, V., Fedorko, R., & Košíková, M. (2021). The use of social media and its impact on the shopping behaviour of Slovak and Italian consumers during the COVID-19 pandemic. *Sustainability*	The article is borrowed from the MDPI database.	The article looks at shopping behaviour among customers. The sample market is Italian and Slovak clientele during the COVID-19 pandemic. The authors examine shopping behaviour among these	The article is essential to the topic as it shows the various advertising techniques applied by e-shops during and after the pandemic.

, *13*(4), 1710. https://doi.org/10.3390/su13041710		clients, targeting specific e-shops during the first wave of the pandemic.	
Saura, J. R. (2021). Using Data Sciences in Digital Marketing: Framework, methods, and performance metrics. *Journal of Innovation & Knowledge*, *6*(2), 92–102. https://doi.org/10.1016/j.jik.2020.08.001	The article was borrowed from the ScienceDirect database.	The article examines the different decision-making practices applied based on the digital marketing environment. There is a scarcity of relevant evidence used to measure advances in improving the	The article is essential to the topic, as it shows the various data management techniques used in marketing practices.

		management of Data Sciences in digital marketing. The results provide an excellent overview of the critical applications of Data Sciences in digital marketing practices and generate key insights linked to developing new data mining discovery techniques.	
/aleri, M., & Baggio, R.	The article was	The article examines	The article is

(2020). Social Network Analysis: Organisational implications in tourism management. *International Journal of Organisational Analysis*, *29*(2), 342–353. https://doi.org/10.1108/ijoa-12-2019-1971	obtained from the Emerald Insight database.	social network analysis, with the tourism industry as the target audience. The article provides an overview of qualitative analysis methodologies and their use to enhance competitiveness in the tourism industry. The methods also account for how these adopted techniques impact data	essential to the topic, as it provides insight into mergers across different economic sectors, based on data collection, analysis, and customer responses.

		collection in other economic sectors.	
wivedi, Y. K., Ismagilova, E., Hughes, D. L., Carlson, J., Filieri, R., Jacobson, J., Jain, V., Karjaluoto, H., Kefi, H., Krishen, A. S., Kumar, V., Rahman, M. M., Raman, R., Rauschnabel, P. A., Rowley, J., Salo, J., Tran, G. A., & Wang, Y. (2021).	The article was borrowed from the ScienceDir ect database	The article indicates that companies use the internet and social media in different ways in business. The reliance on social and digital marketing techniques has presented significant opportunities for top firms through lower costs, increased	The article's significan ce to the topic is evident in its incorpora tion of new advertisin g technique s used by companie s on social media and through digital

Setting the future of digital and social media marketing research: Perspectives and Research Propositions. *International Journal of Information Management*, *59*, 102168. https://doi.org/10.1016/j.ijinfomgt.2020.102168		sales, and improved brand awareness.	marketing .
acobson, J., Gruzd, A., & Hernández-García, Á. (2020). Social Media	The article was borrowed from the ScienceDir	The article provides insight into the benefits of social media	The article's importance to the topic is seen in

Marketing: Who is watching the watchers? *Journal of Retailing and Consumer Services*, *53*, 101774. https://doi.org/10.1016/j.jretconser.2019.03.001	ect database.	towards data that marketers currently use for strategy development and digital marketing practices. On the other hand, the article provides little information on the norms governing the use of social media in marketing. There is a gap in understanding the consumers' comfort with marketers'	the information on which parties are the key beneficiaries of social media marketing practices.

		use of social media data.	
erhausen, D., Miočević, D., Morgan, R. E., & Kleijnen, M. H. P. (2020). The Digital Marketing Capabilities Gap. *Industrial Marketing Management*, *90*, 276–290. https://doi.org/10.1016/j.indmarman.2020.07.022	The article was borrowed from the ScienceDirect database	The article looks at the marketing capabilities gap. The authors review an estimated 129 articles that identify the digital marketing capabilities of a B2B corporation. The authors further claim that the digitisation approach has evolved in the past twenty years, not only in	The article's importance to the topic reflects the benefits of digitisation practices in marketing.

		consumer marketing but also in industrial marketing.	
sai, V. (2019). *Fostering innovation, integration, and inclusion through ...* www.ijtsrd.com. Retrieved April 9, 2023, from https://www.researchgate.net/publication/333709184_Fostering_Innovation_Integration_and_Inclusion_through_Interdisciplinary_Pract	The article was borrowed from the IJTSRD database.	The article looks at the devices companies often use for marketing purposes. Companies apply different trends during the marketing process. Computers brought significant changes to business. There was a shift in marketing	The article's importance is evident in the presentation of the changes companies make to their advertising and marketing techniques.

ices_in_Management		approaches from traditional to digital, targeting a new adaptation of clients towards their products and services.	
ıeung, M. L., Pires, G., & Rosenberger, P. J. (2020). The influence of perceived social media marketing elements on consumer–brand engagement and brand knowledge. *Asia Pacific*	The article was borrowed from the Emerald and Insight database.	The authors examine the influence of perceived elements of social media marketing on consumer-brand engagement. This paper investigates the impact of social media marketing	The article's importance is evident in its analysis of the key elements influencing brand awareness and knowledge.

Journal of Marketing and Logistics, *32*(3), 695–720. https://doi.org/10.1108/apjml-04-2019-0262		elements, including entertainment, interaction, customisation, EWOM, and brand knowledge. The target market was Hong Kong, with the online survey conducted among 214 social media users who indicated their consumption rates of a technology-durable product.	
Wang, C. L. (2021). New	The article was	The article examines the	The article's

Frontiers and Future Directions in Interactive Marketing: Inaugural Editorial. *Journal of Research in Interactive Marketing*, *15*(1), 1–9. https://doi.org/10.1108/jrim-03-2021-270	borrowed from the Emerald and Insight database.	new frontiers and future directions of interactive marketing practices. There has been tremendous growth since the advent of interactive marketing, which has moved beyond traditional forms. The decline of passive broadcast advertising and one-way persuasive communication techniques	importance is seen in its discussion of interactive marketing techniques within businesses.

		has also accompanied the advent of interactive marketing.	
...troni, J., von Briel, F., & Recker, J. (2022). Unpacking the social media–driven innovation capability: How consumer conversations turn into organisational innovations. *Information & Management*, *59*(3), 103267. https://doi.org	The article was borrowed from the Emerald and Insight database.	The article examines consumer conversations on social media, highlighting the possibilities and challenges a company may face in identifying value ideologies in these conversations that could drive successful	The article's importance to the topic is evident in its analysis of the conversational practices companies use when handling business programs.

/10.1016/j.im. 2020.103267		innovations. The authors examine the different approaches that large retailers develop and the new capabilities to leverage in public social media dialogue.	
A., Bahadur, W., Wang, N., Luqman, A., & Khan, A. N. (2020). Improving team innovation performance: Role of Social Media and Team	The article was retrieved from the ScienceDir ect database	The report examines social media practices and how they are used to manage information flow within teams, empowering management	The article is essential to the topic, indicating how companie s improve their innovativ e

Knowledge Management Capabilities. *Technology in Society*, *61*, 101259. https://doi.org/10.1016/j.techsoc.2020.101259		and potentially linking this to innovation. The authors built a model to help test social media's influence on transactive memory systems and team innovation performance.	performance through social media and team knowledge management capabilities.
ean, F. S., Trif, S. M., & Tuleu, D. L. (2019). Customer relationship management capabilities and use of social media	The article was retrieved from the ScienceDirect database	The report examines client relationship management capabilities and the use of social media technology.	The article is essential to illustrating the benefits of social media use to a

technology: Consequences for firm performance. *Journal of Business Research*, *104*, 563–575. https://doi.org/10.1016/j.jbusres.2018.10.047		The authors examine the importance of institutional factors in the adoption of novel technologies and their role in SMT. The key target was to strengthen CRM capabilities, and the impact on a firm's performance has not been investigated.	firm's performance.
ıninger, M.-I., Hammedi, W., & Mahr, D. (2019). The value of	The article was retrieved from the ScienceDir	The authors look at the value of social media in innovation	The article's importance to the topic is

social media for innovation: A capability perspective. *Journal of Business Research*, *95*, 116–127. https://doi.org/10.1016/j.jbusres.2018.10.012	ect database	practices. The authors incorporate strategies managers use to implement innovative ideas. The article also discusses organisational capability theories of innovation. The authors also guide managers in implementing social media strategies within the company.	evident in its discussion of social media's value for business innovation.
ekstra, J. C., & Leeflang, P. S. H. (2020,	The article was retrieved	The article looks at marketing	The importance of this

November 23). *Marketing in the era of Covid-19 - Italian Journal of Marketing*. SpringerLink. Retrieved April 9, 2023, from https://link.springer.com/article/10.1007/s43039-020-00016-3	from the SpringerLink database, sourced from the Italian Journal of Marketing.	practices during the Covid-19 era. The authors discuss the effects of the pandemic on consumer behaviour and elaborate on the outcomes of this disruption of marketing strategies and policies. The crisis also demonstrated changes in consumer behaviour and the impact of marketing approaches	article to the topic lies in changes in customer behaviour during the pandemic and the techniques companies used to market their products and services.

		on the economic downturn.	

Outline

I. Literature synthesis

An estimated 30 sources on the provided topic. The primary target is to illustrate the recent changes in the use of social media in product marketing.

Literature review

This section provides a breakdown of the importance of the selected sources towards the topic. The review is further broken down into;

An introduction: explaining the concepts and facets of social media within an advertising/marketing practice

Social media in product marketing: the section starts by describing the concept and facets of social media and product marketing. It further illustrates the impact of social media marketing towards the client's buying behaviour.

Social media activities: After an overview of consumer communication through social media, this section examines the online strategies companies use in their marketing programs. The section also examines the benefits companies enjoy from social media marketing programs.

Types of applied data: This section covers the data collection techniques companies use in their marketing programs. Further illustrations are offered about CSM and IAP in analysing the marketing programs.

References: This section provides additional sources used to explain the importance and significance of the 30 sources to the topic.

Chapter

The Use of Social Media in Product Marketing

dissertation

Literature Review

Introduction

Social media is used by billions of people globally, making it one of the fastest-growing technologies in this era. It has also permitted people to interact with peers freely and provides numerous platforms for marketers to engage with their clients. Given its dynamic, ever-changing nature, social media's effectiveness as a marketing communications channel has provided marketers with multiple ways to manage their businesses. The use of social media differs from traditional marketing approaches. Most companies in the current market are investing heavily in their social media presence, driven by a recognition of the need to engage with clients through media conversations. The ultimate target is to build a stronger consumer brand.

It is also documented that social media platforms have replaced traditional media. More clients are using them (social media digital platforms) as a source of information on their brands, products, and services. The identified sources are interlinked, demonstrating the various trends in social media platforms' reliance on advertisements. Clients respond differently depending on the type of social media a company uses to advertise its products. Such instances often occur because a particular social media platform attracts a distinct customer segment, thereby indirectly affecting sales revenue.

Social Media in Product Marketing

This literature review aims to demonstrate the future of social media in consumer product marketing. The identified sources will be used through a deductive approach, with an attempt to review recent scholarly material on social media marketing. Different interpretations will be applied to examine the dynamic role of social media within a digitised business environment in promoting and branding consumer goods. In the long run, a comprehensive analysis will demonstrate that social media is a significant player in the current marketing scene. According to Siriwardana (2020), the creation of social networking platforms such as Facebook contributed to the

Economics for Academic and Business. J. Safo popularity of social media. Similarly, terms like Web 2.0 were first used in the era of Facebook's birth (2003-2004), describing the novel utilisation of the internet as a platform where people could freely express their ideas.

Social Media and Consumer Communication Techniques

The identified sources help show that social media has significantly shifted how marketers and consumers communicate. However, a pivotal question is how these media platforms have transformed the world of e-marketing. The current business environment has also changed due to the global pandemic, which severely affected the world and left people with no option but to find innovative ways to operate. The results have further demonstrated that social media has positively affected how people execute their businesses.

Social Media Marketing Activities

Most institutions in the current business era are using online marketing strategies, such as relying on blogger endorsements. To a certain extent, advertisements are included on media sites, and user-generated content is managed to build brand awareness among existing clientele. Kavak *et al.* (2020) define social media as internet-based apps that enable the production and sharing of user-generated content. Because of the interactive traits that support knowledge sharing, companies have found better ways to disclose brand information. Notably, social media includes blogs, internet forums, and social networking sites. When analysing the marketing techniques used by luxury brands, it is necessary to incorporate concepts such as customisation, reputation, interaction, and entertainment, as they help create product significance, brand identity, and the client's purchase intention (Erragchaa & Babay, 2022). Most activities that require community marketing are shaped by the different interactions between events and individuals' mental stability. These products are seen as external factors to the user.

The identified sources show that people have always experienced similar service activities, which has also triggered different ideas and feelings regarding a particular event. The outcomes for users and consumers have always been distinct. Therefore, as we analyse future marketing activities, competition is likely to be based on brand marketing activities, with these activities aimed at delivering sensory stimulation and themes that offer clients more extraordinary experiences. Currently, brands are

Economics for Academic and Business. J. Safo offering clients high-quality features while also focusing on delivering an extraordinary client experience. The ultimate goal is to have the product purchased by more people in a particular market.

Type of Applied Data

Heavy reliance on current information will not yield a desirable conclusion on what may be required for future practices. Still, identifying the marketing gaps provides a platform for integrating the missing information on the topic. There are significant differences among the social media platforms currently used by companies, as these platforms directly influence the target market a firm reaches. Similarly, there is a need to address issues with the traditional marketing techniques a company uses. Such data offers an opportunity to create a particular sequence of the market trends experienced by a given company. For instance, using CSM content will help a researcher measure the rate at which consumers perceive social media marketing practices. Nevertheless, their perception of a product will heavily influence their purchasing decision. Therefore, a successful marketing campaign will be achieved by relying on technology that targets different consumer clusters, regardless of location.

The IAP is another instrument that provides information on a client's acceptance of new technology. The IAP is a framework for managing an innovation process. The ideologies are applied across the identified sources, illustrating the different steps a manager can take to realise benefits or innovation within the market. Most of these practices have been used in the post-COVID-19 era, with companies seeking new techniques to market their products and maintain relatively high customer retention rates. The concept of social media advertising has advanced, creating multiple platforms where producers and consumers stay in touch and share different types of information. Marketers and retailers constantly use these platforms to reach clients. These developments have also given rise to multiple powerful search engines that help consumers find the information they need about these items. Reference List.

Erragcha, N. & Babay, H. (2022). "Social Media, marketing practices, and consumer behaviour," *Research Anthology on Social Media Advertising and Building Consumer Relationships*, pp. 34–52.

Kavak, B., Özdemir, N. & Erol-Boyacı, G. (2020). "A literature review of social media for marketing,"

Economics for Academic and Business. J. Safo *Advances in Marketing, Customer Relationship Management, and E-Services*, pp. 67–96.

Siriwardana, A. (2020). “Social Media Marketing: A literature review on consumer products,” *SSRN Electronic Journal* [Preprint].

.

Chapter 4
The Concept of a Firm's Cost Structure

The Concept of a Firm's Cost Structure

A firm's cost structure refers to how a business organises, incurs, and manages the different costs associated with producing and selling goods or services. Every business, regardless of its size or industry, must use resources such as labour, raw materials, machinery, buildings, electricity, transportation, technology, and managerial services to produce its output (Shapiro et al., 2024). These resources incur costs, and understanding how those costs behave as production levels change is essential for effective business decision-making. A firm's cost structure therefore provides an important framework for understanding profitability, pricing, production decisions, budgeting, and resource allocation.

Cost structures differ considerably among businesses. For example, a manufacturing company may have substantial expenditure on machinery, factories, raw materials, electricity, and labour. In contrast, a consulting firm may have relatively low expenditure on physical materials but high expenditure on salaries, professional services, office space, and technology (Shapiro et al., 2024). Similarly, an online business may have significant technology and marketing costs while having relatively low physical production costs. A firm's cost structure is influenced by its industry, size, technology, production methods, scale of operations, and management decisions.

The major concepts used to understand a firm's cost structure include fixed costs, variable costs, total costs, average costs, and marginal costs. Although these costs are related, they have different meanings and behave differently as production changes. Understanding these distinctions enables managers to determine the most efficient level of production, establish appropriate prices, assess profitability, and make informed short-run and long-run decisions.

Fixed Costs

Fixed costs are costs that do not change with the level of output within a particular period. In other words, a firm must generally incur these costs regardless of whether it produces a large quantity, a small quantity, or temporarily produces nothing. Fixed costs are therefore associated with maintaining the firm's capacity to operate rather than directly with the number of units produced.

Examples of fixed costs include rent for business premises, salaries of permanent administrative employees, insurance premiums, property taxes, depreciation of buildings and machinery, and certain licensing fees. For example, suppose a bakery rents a building for $3,000 per month. Whether the bakery produces 500 loaves or 5,000 loaves during the month, the monthly rent remains $3,000 under the existing rental agreement. The rent is therefore a fixed cost.

Another example is the annual insurance premium paid by a manufacturing company. If the company pays $24,000 per year for insurance, this amount generally remains unchanged regardless of whether production is high or low during that year (Halliday et al., 2025). Similarly, a hotel may have to pay for its building lease and certain administrative salaries regardless of the number of rooms occupied.

Fixed costs are particularly important because they create financial obligations that businesses must meet even when sales are low. A firm with very high fixed costs may benefit significantly from economies of scale when production increases because the fixed cost can be spread over a larger number of units. However, such a firm may also face greater financial risk when demand falls.

It is important to recognise that fixed costs are fixed only within a relevant range and over a specified period. For example, a factory's rent may remain unchanged while production increases from 10,000 to 20,000 units. However, if production expands substantially and the firm needs another factory, rent will increase. Therefore, fixed costs are not permanently fixed; rather, they remain constant over a particular range of production and time.

Variable Costs

Variable costs are costs that change directly or substantially with the level of output. As a firm produces more units, its variable costs generally increase. When production decreases, variable costs generally fall. These costs are directly related to the firm's production activity (Shapiro et al., 2024). Common examples include raw materials, packaging materials, production-related wages, sales commissions, fuel used for deliveries, and certain utility costs. For example, consider a clothing manufacturer producing shirts. The more shirts it produces, the more fabric, buttons, thread, labels, and packaging materials it needs. These materials therefore represent variable costs.

Suppose a manufacturer spends $8 on materials and direct labour for every shirt produced. If the company produces 1,000 shirts, the total cost would be approximately $8,000. If production increases to 2,000 shirts, the variable costs would increase to approximately $16,000, assuming the cost per shirt remains constant. A restaurant provides another useful example. The cost of food ingredients such as meat, vegetables, flour, cooking oil, and beverages increases as the restaurant serves more customers. If the restaurant serves 100 customers, it will generally require fewer ingredients than when it serves 500 customers. These costs therefore vary with the level of business activity.

Variable costs are important when managers make short-run production decisions because they help determine whether producing additional units is financially worthwhile. A business must consider whether the revenue generated from additional sales is sufficient to cover additional variable costs and contribute to fixed costs and profit (Shapiro et al., 2024). However, variable costs do not necessarily increase at the same rate forever. Bulk purchasing may reduce the cost per unit, while overtime wages, material scarcity, or capacity constraints may increase costs as production expands. Thus, the relationship between output and variable costs can change depending on operating conditions.

Total Costs

Total cost is the total cost incurred by a firm in producing a given level of output. It combines fixed costs and variable costs. The basic relationship is:

Total Cost = Total Fixed Cost + Total Variable Cost

For example, assume a furniture manufacturer has monthly fixed costs of $20,000. If it produces 1,000 tables and incurs variable costs of $30,000, its total cost will be $50,000.

If production increases to 2,000 tables and variable costs rise to $60,000 while fixed costs remain at $20,000, total cost becomes $80,000.

This illustrates an important characteristic of total cost: because fixed costs remain constant in the short run, changes in total cost are primarily caused by changes in variable costs. When output is zero, a firm may still incur fixed costs. For example, a factory that temporarily stops production may still have to pay rent, insurance, security, and administrative expenses.

Total cost is important for determining whether a firm is profitable. A firm's profit can be expressed as total revenue minus total cost. Therefore, managers need to know their total costs when evaluating the financial performance of a product or business activity. For example, if a company generates total revenue of $100,000 and its total costs are $75,000, its accounting profit before other applicable adjustments would be $25,000. If total costs increase to $110,000 while revenue remains unchanged, the firm would experience a loss. Total cost therefore provides an overall picture of the resources used in production and helps businesses establish budgets, determine profitability, and evaluate alternative production plans.

Average Costs

Average cost refers to the cost of producing one unit of output. It is calculated by dividing total cost by the quantity of output produced.

Average Cost = Total Cost ÷ Quantity of Output

Average cost can also be divided into average fixed cost and average variable cost.

Average Fixed Cost = Total Fixed Cost ÷ Quantity of Output

Average Variable Cost = Total Variable Cost ÷ Quantity of Output

For example, suppose a company has total costs of $50,000 and produces 5,000 units. Its average cost is $10 per unit. This means that, on average, each unit costs the firm $10 to produce.

Average cost is particularly important for pricing and profitability decisions. If a firm sells its product for $15 per unit and its average cost is $10, it appears to have a $5 per-unit contribution to profit, assuming all relevant costs have been included in the calculation.

One important feature of average fixed cost is that it falls as output increases. For example, if a factory has fixed costs of $20,000, producing 1,000 units means fixed cost per unit is $20. If production increases to 2,000 units, fixed cost per unit falls to $10. At 4,000 units, it falls to $5. This illustrates why businesses often seek to increase production and sales when they have substantial fixed costs.

Average variable cost may initially decline because of increased efficiency but may eventually rise if the firm experiences capacity constraints, overtime costs, congestion, or diminishing productivity (Halliday et al., 2025). Average total cost can therefore decline initially as fixed costs are spread over more units, reach a minimum point, and potentially rise at higher levels of production.

For example, a manufacturing firm may find that producing 1,000 units results in an average cost of $20 per unit, while producing 5,000 units reduces average cost to $12 per unit. However, if production is expanded to 15,000 units, overcrowding, equipment breakdowns, overtime payments, and management difficulties may raise the average cost to $14. This illustrates the relationship between production scale and cost efficiency.

Marginal Costs

Marginal cost is the additional cost incurred from producing one additional unit of output. It focuses on the change in total cost resulting from a change in production.

Marginal Cost = Change in Total Cost ÷ Change in Quantity of Output

For example, suppose a bakery produces 1,000 cakes at a total cost of $10,000. If producing an additional 100 cakes increases total cost to $10,700, the marginal cost of those additional cakes is $7 per cake.

Marginal cost differs from average cost because it refers to the additional cost of producing an extra unit of output, rather than the cost of existing output. This makes marginal cost particularly important for short-run production decisions (Shapiro et al., 2024). Consider a restaurant that normally serves 200 customers per evening. If serving 20 additional customers requires $200 in additional food, labour, and other costs, the marginal cost is $10 per additional customer. If each additional customer

Economics for Academic and Business. J. Safo generates $25 in revenue, serving those customers would generally improve the firm's profitability, provided there are no other relevant constraints.

Marginal cost is also closely associated with the law of diminishing marginal returns. In the short run, some inputs such as factory size or major equipment may be fixed (McGuigan et al., 2013). As more variable inputs, such as labour, are added to fixed resources, workers may initially become more productive. Eventually, however, overcrowding or capacity limitations may cause additional workers to contribute less additional output. Consequently, marginal cost may initially fall and then increase.

Managers pay considerable attention to marginal cost when deciding whether to expand production (Shapiro et al., 2024). If the marginal revenue from selling an additional unit exceeds the marginal cost of producing it, producing that additional unit can increase profit. Conversely, if marginal cost exceeds marginal revenue, increasing output may reduce profit. Thus, marginal analysis is an important tool for optimising production decisions.

Relationship Between the Different Cost Concepts

Although fixed, variable, total, average, and marginal costs are distinct concepts, they are closely interconnected. Fixed costs remain constant within the relevant production range, while variable costs vary with output. Total cost combines these two categories (McGuigan et al., 2013). Average cost is the total cost per unit, while marginal cost is the additional cost of producing one more unit.

For example, imagine a small juice-processing business with monthly fixed costs of $10,000. Its variable cost is $2 for every bottle produced.
If the business produces 1,000 bottles, its variable cost is $2,000 and total cost is $12,000. The average cost per bottle is therefore $12. If production increases to 5,000 bottles, variable costs rise to $10,000, and total cost becomes $20,000. Average cost falls to $4 per bottle. The reduction occurs because the $10,000 fixed cost is now distributed across 5,000 bottles rather than only 1,000.

If producing an additional bottle requires another $2 in variable resources, the marginal cost of that additional bottle is approximately $2, assuming no change in production conditions.
This example demonstrates why a firm's cost structure influences its production strategy. A business with high fixed costs may need high production and sales volumes to spread those costs efficiently. A business with low fixed costs but high variable costs may have greater flexibility during

periods of weak demand because its costs fall more substantially when production declines.

Importance of Cost Structure to Business Decisions

Understanding cost structure is essential for several aspects of business management. First, it supports pricing decisions. A firm needs to understand its costs before establishing a sustainable price (Mowen & Hansen, 2014). Pricing below total cost for an extended period may result in losses. However, firms may sometimes accept prices below average total cost temporarily if prices cover relevant variable costs and contribute toward fixed costs.

Second, cost structure assists with budgeting and financial planning. Managers can estimate how much the firm will spend at different levels of production and sales (Mowen & Hansen, 2014). This allows them to forecast profits and identify potential cash-flow pressures. Third, cost analysis supports break-even analysis. The break-even point is the level of output or sales at which total revenue equals total cost. At this point, the firm makes neither a profit nor a loss. Businesses with high fixed costs generally need higher sales volumes to reach break-even.

Fourth, cost structure affects decisions concerning economies of scale. Economies of scale occur when average cost decreases as production expands. This may happen because fixed costs are distributed across more units, employees specialise, purchasing becomes more efficient, or technology improves productivity. On the other hand, firms can eventually experience diseconomies of scale (Mowen & Hansen, 2014). These occur when expansion increases average costs. Large organisations may experience communication problems, bureaucratic delays, coordination difficulties, challenges in employee supervision, and other inefficiencies.

Cost structure is also important when firms consider outsourcing, automation, expansion, or entering new markets. For example, a company may compare the fixed cost of purchasing an automated production machine with the variable labour costs associated with manual production. Although automation may require substantial initial investment, it could reduce variable costs over time and lower average costs if production volume is sufficiently high.

Business Example: A Manufacturing Firm

Consider a company producing bottled water. The company may pay $15,000 per month for factory rent, insurance, administrative salaries, and equipment depreciation. These are largely fixed costs. It must pay them even if production is temporarily low (Garrison et al., 2003). The company also incurs variable costs, including bottles, labels, caps, and water treatment materials, as well as electricity for production, packaging, and distribution. If the company produces more bottles, these costs increase.

Suppose production of 10,000 bottles results in total variable costs of $20,000. Total cost would therefore be $35,000. The average cost would be $3.50 per bottle. If production increases to 20,000 bottles and variable costs increase to $40,000, total cost becomes $55,000. Average cost falls to $2.75 per bottle because the same $15,000 fixed cost is spread over twice as many bottles.

If producing an additional 1,000 bottles increases total cost by $2,000, the marginal cost is $2 per bottle. If the company can sell each additional bottle at a price above its marginal cost while satisfying market demand and capacity constraints, increasing production may be financially beneficial (Garrison et al., 2003). This example demonstrates how the different cost concepts interact in an actual business. It also shows why managers should not consider only total costs when making production decisions. Average and marginal costs provide additional information about efficiency and the financial consequences of increasing output.

Conclusion

To summarise, a firm's cost structure describes the nature and behaviour of costs associated with production and operations. Understanding costs helps businesses set prices, forecast profits, allocate resources, and make effective production decisions. Fixed costs remain constant within a relevant production range, including rent, insurance, and administrative salaries. Variable costs change with output and include raw materials, packaging, and production labour. Total costs combine fixed and variable costs. Average cost represents the cost per unit, while marginal cost measures the additional cost of producing one more unit. Understanding these costs helps firms evaluate efficiency, control expenses, identify economies of scale, determine profitability, and make informed investment decisions. Effective cost management strengthens competitiveness, improves resource utilisation, supports sustainable growth, and enables firms to respond effectively to changes in demand and market conditions.

References

Garrison, R. H., Noreen, E. W., Brewer, P. C., & Montague, N. R. (2003). *Managerial accounting*. New York: McGraw-Hill/Irwin. https://www.mheducation.com/highered/product/managerial-accounting-for-managers-noreen.html?viewOption=student#mh-ecomm-he-product-accordion-2007874096-heading-mh-ecomm-accordion-list-7f3a086061

Halliday, S. D., & Madhurika Mamunuru, S. (2025). Updating our approach to intermediate microeconomics. *The American Economist*, *70*(2), 295-314. https://ideas.repec.org/a/sae/amerec/v70y2025i2p295-314.html

McGuigan, J. R., Moyer, R. C., & Harris, F. H. D. (2013). Managerial economics: applications, strategies and tactics. Nelson Education.

Mowen, M. M., & Hansen, D. R. (2014). Cornerstones of managerial accounting. *(No Title)*.

Shapiro, D., MacDonald, D., & Greenlaw, S. A. (2024). *Principles of Macroeconomics 3e*. VK Publications.

Chapter 5

The Role of Government in a Mixed Economy

The Role of Government in a Mixed Economy

Meaning and Characteristics of a Mixed Economy

A mixed economy incorporates elements of both capitalism and government planning. In a predominantly market-based economy, private individuals and businesses own most resources and make production and investment decisions. Prices are determined mainly by demand and supply, and profit provides an incentive for businesses to produce goods and services efficiently. In contrast, in a centrally planned economy, the government has extensive control over resources, production, prices, and distribution. A mixed economy lies between these two systems. Private businesses are allowed to operate and compete, while the government establishes rules and provides services considered essential to society. The government may own and operate enterprises in strategic sectors while allowing private firms to operate in other industries.

Several characteristics distinguish a mixed economy. First, private property and private enterprise are generally permitted. Individuals can own businesses, land, and other productive assets. Second, markets play a major role in determining prices and allocating resources. Third, governments regulate economic activities to protect consumers, workers, businesses, and the environment. Fourth, governments provide public goods and merit goods such as national defence, public education, infrastructure, and certain healthcare services. Finally, governments redistribute income through taxation, social security programmes, subsidies, and other welfare policies. The mixed economy therefore recognises that markets are useful mechanisms for allocating resources but may need to be complemented by government action.

Why Governments Intervene in Markets

Correcting Market Failure

One of the most important reasons for government intervention is market failure. Market failure occurs when the free operation of markets does not result in an efficient allocation of resources. Several forms of market failure justify government intervention. One major example is externalities. An externality occurs when an economic activity affects third parties who are not directly involved in the transaction. Negative externalities include air pollution, water pollution, noise, and environmental degradation. A factory may produce goods at a private cost while imposing pollution costs on surrounding communities. Because the producer does not bear the full social cost, the market may produce more of the good than is socially desirable.

Governments can address negative externalities through environmental regulations, pollution taxes, emissions standards, and other policies. For example, a government may impose a tax on activities that generate carbon emissions. Such a tax can encourage firms and consumers to consider environmental costs when making economic decisions. Positive externalities provide another reason for intervention. Positive externalities occur when an activity generates benefits for people who are not directly involved in the transaction. Education and vaccination are common examples. An educated population may be more productive, healthier, and better able to participate in democratic institutions, benefiting society as a whole. Similarly, vaccination can protect not only vaccinated individuals but also other members of the community. Because individuals may consider only their private benefits, the market may provide less education or vaccination than is socially desirable. Governments can therefore provide subsidies or directly supply these services.

Provision of Public Goods

Governments intervene because markets may fail to provide sufficient public goods. Public goods have two important characteristics: non-rivalry and non-excludability. Non-rivalry means that one person's consumption does not significantly reduce the amount available to others. Non-excludability means that it is difficult or costly to prevent people from benefiting from the good once it is provided.

National defence is a classic example. Once a country is protected by national defence, it is difficult to exclude particular citizens from receiving the benefit. Street lighting and certain forms of public infrastructure can also have public-good characteristics.

Private businesses may be unwilling to provide such goods because they cannot charge every beneficiary. This creates a free-rider problem, where individuals can benefit without paying. Government taxation allows society to finance the provision of public goods collectively.

Reducing Income and Wealth Inequality

Another important reason for government intervention is the unequal distribution of income and wealth. Market economies reward individuals according to factors such as skills, education, asset ownership, productivity, and demand for particular occupations. Although these incentives can encourage work, investment, and innovation, they can also produce substantial inequalities.

Some households may lack sufficient income to obtain adequate food, housing, healthcare, or education. Governments can reduce extreme inequality through progressive taxation, social protection programmes, unemployment benefits, pensions, cash transfers, food assistance, and subsidised public services.

Redistribution is not intended merely to transfer income from one group to another. It can also promote social stability and improve equality of opportunity. For example, providing affordable education to low-income households can help children develop skills that enable them to participate more effectively in the labour market.

Protecting Consumers

Markets do not always guarantee that consumers receive safe, high-quality, and accurately represented products. Businesses may possess more information about their products than consumers. This creates information asymmetry. For example, consumers may not know whether a used vehicle is mechanically reliable or whether a financial product carries significant risks. Without regulation, firms might exploit information advantages by selling unsafe, defective, or misleading products. Governments therefore establish consumer protection laws, product safety standards, labelling requirements, advertising regulations, competition policies, and financial-sector regulations. These measures can improve consumer confidence and reduce exploitation.

Protecting Workers

Government intervention is also important in labour markets. Employers and employees do not always have equal bargaining power. Workers may accept low wages or unsafe conditions because they have limited employment alternatives. Governments can establish minimum wage laws, occupational health and safety standards, working-hour regulations, maternity protections, anti-discrimination laws, and employment rights. Such measures can improve working conditions and protect vulnerable workers.

However, governments must balance worker protection with the need to maintain employment opportunities. Excessively high labour costs or rigid employment regulations may discourage firms from hiring workers. Therefore, labour-market intervention needs to be carefully designed.

Maintaining Economic Stability

Markets can experience economic fluctuations. Economies may move through periods of rapid growth, inflation, unemployment, recession, and financial instability. Government intervention can help reduce the severity of these fluctuations. Fiscal policy involves government decisions concerning taxation and public expenditure. During a recession, the government may increase public spending or reduce taxes to stimulate aggregate demand. During periods of excessive inflation, it may reduce spending or increase taxes to moderate demand.

Monetary policy, usually conducted by a central bank, influences interest rates, credit conditions, and the money supply. Higher interest rates can reduce excessive demand and inflationary pressure, while lower interest rates can encourage borrowing, investment, and consumption during weak economic conditions. Macroeconomic intervention therefore seeks to promote economic stability, employment, sustainable growth, and price stability.

Major Roles of Government in a Mixed Economy

Regulation of Economic Activity

Governments establish laws and regulations that define how businesses operate. Regulation may cover competition, employment, environmental protection, financial markets, product safety, taxation, and corporate governance. Competition policy is particularly important because monopolies and dominant firms may exploit consumers by charging high prices, reducing output, limiting choice, or preventing competitors from entering the market. Competition authorities can investigate anti-competitive practices, regulate mergers, and prevent abuse of market power. Effective regulation can create a fairer business environment in which firms compete based on quality, efficiency, innovation, and price.

Provision of Infrastructure

Governments play a significant role in providing infrastructure such as roads, bridges, ports, electricity systems, water networks, public transport facilities, schools, and hospitals. Infrastructure supports private-sector activity by reducing transportation costs, improving connectivity, facilitating trade, and increasing productivity. Infrastructure investment can also promote regional development. Roads and electricity connections can enable businesses in rural or less-developed areas to access markets and expand production. Although private companies can provide some infrastructure, government involvement is often necessary where projects have large social benefits, high initial costs, long payback periods, or natural-monopoly characteristics.

Provision of Education and Healthcare

Education and healthcare are important areas of government intervention because they generate both private and social benefits. Education increases human capital, improves productivity, and can contribute to technological development. Healthcare improves labour productivity and quality of life while reducing the spread of disease. If these services were determined entirely by market forces, low-income households might consume too little because they

Economics for Academic and Business. J. Safo could not afford them. Governments can therefore finance, regulate, or directly provide education and healthcare. Government provision also supports equality of opportunity. Individuals should have a reasonable opportunity to develop their abilities regardless of their parents' income.

Redistribution Through Taxation and Welfare

Taxation is one of the government's most important economic instruments. Governments collect revenue through income taxes, corporate taxes, consumption taxes, property taxes, customs duties, and other forms of taxation. Tax revenue finances public services and infrastructure while also enabling governments to redistribute income. Progressive taxation requires individuals with higher incomes to pay a greater proportion of their income in taxes.

Governments can complement taxation with social welfare programmes. These may include pensions, unemployment support, disability assistance, child benefits, food assistance, and housing programmes. Such policies can reduce poverty and protect vulnerable groups.

Promotion of Economic Growth and Development

Governments can promote economic growth by investing in infrastructure, education, healthcare, research and development, technology, and skills development. They may also create policies that encourage entrepreneurship and investment. Governments can provide tax incentives, grants, credit programmes, industrial policies, export support, and special economic zones to encourage business development. However, such policies need to be carefully evaluated because subsidies and incentives can become costly if they support inefficient firms indefinitely.

Environmental Protection

Economic production can create environmental costs. Governments have an important role in ensuring that economic growth does not cause excessive environmental damage.

Environmental policies can include pollution taxes, carbon pricing, emissions standards, environmental impact assessments, conservation laws, renewable-energy incentives, and restrictions on environmentally harmful activities. These policies attempt to align private incentives with social interests. Businesses can still produce and earn profits, but they are encouraged to account for environmental costs.

Advantages of Government Intervention

Correction of Market Failures

The major advantage of government intervention is that it can correct market failures. Where markets underprovide public goods, create harmful externalities, or fail to protect consumers, government action can improve resource allocation. For example, environmental regulations can reduce pollution, while subsidies for education can increase investment in human capital. Such interventions can increase social welfare even when they restrict some market activities.

Reduction of Poverty and Inequality

Government intervention can improve living standards among disadvantaged groups. Progressive taxation and welfare programmes can redistribute income and ensure that vulnerable households have access to necessities. Public education and healthcare can also reduce inequalities by providing services that would otherwise be unaffordable to some groups.

Reducing extreme inequality can promote social cohesion and provide greater equality of opportunity.

Protection of Consumers and Workers

Government regulations can protect consumers from unsafe products and misleading business practices. Labour laws can improve workplace safety, prevent discrimination, and establish minimum employment standards. These protections can improve confidence in markets. Consumers are more likely to participate in markets when they trust that products and services meet reasonable standards.

Provision of Essential Services

Government provision ensures that services with significant social benefits are available even when they are not highly profitable. This is particularly important for services such as public health, education, sanitation, national defence, and infrastructure. Such services contribute to long-term economic development and social welfare.

Economic Stability

Government fiscal and monetary policies can reduce unemployment, control inflation, and respond to economic crises. During recessions, government spending can support aggregate demand and employment. During periods of overheating, restrictive policies can help control inflation. Government intervention is particularly important during financial crises when the failure of major institutions could affect the entire economy.

Promotion of Long-Term Development

Markets may sometimes focus on short-term profits rather than long-term social benefits. Governments can undertake investments whose returns are realised over many years, such as education, infrastructure, research, climate adaptation, and public health. These investments can increase the economy's productive capacity and improve future living standards.

Disadvantages of Government Intervention

Government Failure

Government intervention does not always produce better outcomes. Government failure occurs when government policies result in inefficient or undesirable outcomes.

Governments may lack accurate information about consumers, businesses, production costs, or future economic conditions. As a result, policies may be poorly designed or have unintended consequences. For example, a price ceiling intended to make housing affordable may reduce landlords' incentive to provide rental properties. If the price is set below the market equilibrium price for an extended period, shortages can occur.

Bureaucracy and Administrative Costs

Government programmes require administrative systems, employees, monitoring, and enforcement. These activities can be expensive. Excessive bureaucracy may slow decision-making and create unnecessary procedures for businesses and citizens. When regulations become overly complex, firms may spend substantial resources on compliance rather than on productive activities.

Reduced Economic Efficiency

Intervention can reduce market efficiency if regulations are excessive or poorly designed. For example, strict regulations may increase production costs and discourage businesses from investing. Similarly, high taxes may reduce incentives to work, save, invest, or undertake entrepreneurial activities. The extent of these effects depends on the type and level of taxation and the structure of the economy.

Distortion of Market Prices

Taxes, subsidies, and price controls can distort market signals. Prices normally communicate information about scarcity and consumer preferences. When governments artificially influence prices, consumers and producers may make decisions that do not reflect actual economic conditions. For example, subsidies can encourage excessive production of a particular good, while price controls can create shortages or surpluses.

Risk of Political Interference

Government economic decisions may be influenced by political objectives rather than economic efficiency. Politicians may support policies that provide immediate benefits to voters even if they create long-term costs. For example, governments may increase subsidies or public spending before elections. Such policies can increase fiscal deficits or create economic distortions. Political influence may also result in government contracts or support being directed toward politically connected businesses rather than the most productive firms.

Corruption and Misuse of Public Resources

Large government budgets and public procurement systems can create opportunities for corruption. If public officials misuse resources for personal gain, taxpayers receive less value from government expenditure. Corruption can discourage investment, increase project costs, reduce public trust, and weaken institutions.

Dependency and Reduced Incentives

Welfare programmes can protect vulnerable individuals, but poorly designed programmes may create dependency if benefits significantly reduce incentives to seek employment or increase income. This does not mean that social protection is inherently harmful. Rather, welfare systems should be designed so that support protects people from poverty while encouraging participation in education, training, and employment where possible.

Evaluation of Government Intervention

The effectiveness of government intervention depends largely on the nature of the problem, the policy instrument selected, the quality of institutions, and the government's ability to implement and monitor policies. Government intervention is most justified where market failure is substantial, and the benefits of intervention are likely to exceed its costs. For example, controlling pollution can generate significant social benefits because environmental damage may impose costs on millions of people. Similarly, public investment in basic education can produce long-term

Economics for Academic and Business. J. Safo benefits that individual households may not fully consider.

However, intervention should not automatically replace market mechanisms. Markets are powerful tools for allocating resources because prices provide information and incentives. Competition can encourage firms to reduce costs, improve quality, and innovate. Excessive government control can weaken these incentives.

The most effective mixed economies therefore seek an appropriate balance between market forces and government intervention. Governments should establish clear rules, correct major market failures, provide essential public goods, protect vulnerable groups, and maintain macroeconomic stability while allowing private businesses sufficient freedom to innovate and compete.

The principle of proportionality is important. The government should select the least distortionary policy that can effectively address a particular problem. For example, rather than banning an environmentally harmful activity completely, a government might impose a pollution tax that encourages firms to reduce emissions while allowing them flexibility in choosing how to do so. Policy evaluation is also essential. Governments should assess whether intervention is achieving its intended objectives and whether the benefits exceed the costs. Policies should be modified or removed when they become ineffective or unnecessarily costly.

Government Intervention and Economic Development

Government intervention is particularly significant in developing economies. Private markets may not provide sufficient infrastructure, education, healthcare, credit, or technological investment. Governments can therefore play a major role in creating the conditions necessary for economic development. Investment in roads, electricity, telecommunications, schools, and healthcare can improve productivity and attract private investment. Government policies can also support small and medium-sized enterprises, entrepreneurship, agricultural development, and industrialisation.

However, developing countries may face greater risks of government failure because of limited administrative capacity, weak institutions, corruption, and constrained public finances. Poorly designed interventions can result in wasted resources and high public debt. Therefore, government intervention in developing economies should emphasise institutional quality, transparency, accountability, evidence-based policymaking, and efficient use of public resources.

The Appropriate Balance Between Government and Markets

The central issue in a mixed economy is finding the appropriate balance between government and markets. Neither extreme provides a universally effective solution. A completely free market may generate innovation and efficiency but can also produce inequality, externalities, inadequate public goods, and economic instability. A completely government-controlled economy may promote certain social objectives but can suffer from weak incentives, bureaucracy, shortages, inefficiency, and limited consumer choice.

A mixed economy attempts to combine the strengths of both systems. Markets can handle many ordinary economic decisions efficiently, while government intervention can address areas where market outcomes are inadequate. For example, private businesses may efficiently produce food, clothing, electronics, and many consumer services because competition provides strong incentives to be efficient. At the same time, government may regulate food safety, environmental standards, labour conditions, and consumer protection.

Similarly, private healthcare and education providers can operate alongside government-funded schools and hospitals. This creates choice while ensuring that essential services remain accessible to individuals who cannot afford private alternatives. The appropriate balance can also change over time. During a financial crisis, governments may need to intervene more extensively to prevent economic collapse. During periods of strong economic growth, governments may reduce certain temporary interventions and allow market forces to play a greater role.

Chapter 6

Artificial Intelligence in Accounting and Auditing – Ethical Use of AI in the Field of Accounting and Auditing

Artificial Intelligence in Accounting and Auditing – Ethical Use of AI in the Field of Accounting and Auditing

Introduction

In the accounting and auditing field, those preparing to work in it may include accountants, auditors, and students. This community is facing a

Economics for Academic and Business. J. Safo serious problem due to changes in the methods used to carry out work in this field. The use of artificial intelligence (AI) in accounting and auditing is the key issue here. AI is being used in this field to perform several tasks, such as checking financial data, preparing reports, analyzing transactions, and supporting audit activities. Such a change is transforming how accountants and auditors perform their work and is happening swiftly.

This is just one of the many advantages of AI, enabling accountants to operate faster and minimize errors. AI can quickly review large volumes of financial data, saving humans time that could otherwise be spent performing such tasks. This increases the ease of auditing to detect issues and errors and to manage risks better. AI also has its challenges. One key issue is trust, and people tend not to trust the results produced or processed by machines. AI also has ethical implications, and such systems may produce incorrect results or biased output when not well controlled.

A concern about the role of human accountants, in which AI performs their routine and simple tasks, is alarming. This means that, to remain relevant in their practice, accountants must acquire new skills, become tech-savvy, and embrace AI to avoid being overshadowed by it. This also implies the creation of clear guidelines for firms' responsible use of AI. The source for this paper provides insights on this matter by illustrating how AI is incorporated into auditing, highlighting the associated risks, and outlining the rationale for ensuring auditors are ready and trained to apply AI systems effectively in their duties.

Annotated Bibliography

Li, Y., & Goel, S. (2025). Artificial intelligence auditability and auditor readiness for auditing artificial intelligence systems. *International Journal of Accounting Information Systems*, *56*, 100739. https://doi.org/10.1016/j.accinf.2025.100739

Description Paragraph

The article explores the use of Artificial Intelligence (AI) in auditing and the role of the auditor in utilizing AI technologies for their work. One of the key themes of the article is auditability, defined as the degree to which an AI system can be understood, examined, verified, and assessed by auditors. The authors note that one key consideration for auditability is that auditors are expected to reach reliable, trustworthy conclusions based on evidence. Auditors must possess adequate knowledge of how AI systems

Economics for Academic and Business. J. Safo function and how they create audit evidence. The article thus not only discusses the advantages of AI, but also the various hurdles encountered by auditors who are required to rely on complex technological systems.

Given its capacity for speedy and effective processing of vast amounts of information, artificial intelligence has emerged as a powerful tool in the auditor's arsenal. Conventional auditing can encompass thousands or millions of transactions, financial records, paperwork, and other organizational information. This is a great deal of information to go through by hand, which can be time-consuming and labour-intensive. By analyzing vast amounts of data, detecting anomalous transactions, identifying patterns, and flagging items that may require further investigation, AI can help auditors. This can help auditors carry out their duties more efficiently while devoting more time and resources to areas of the audit that require greater professional judgment and pose greater risk.

One important use of AI in auditing is data analysis. In financial matters, AI systems can process vast amounts of data, financial and non-financial, and uncover connections or patterns that may not be apparent to a human auditor. An AI system can also review transactions to detect any irregular payment patterns, unexpected fluctuations in account balances, duplicate transactions, or activities that vary significantly from the norm. Such capabilities can help auditors identify potential errors, fraud, or areas of increased audit risk. AI can analyze significantly larger datasets than traditional sampling methods, enabling auditors to examine more data. This can help ensure that the scope of the audit procedures is expanded and provides auditors with more evidence to make their professional judgments.

AI can also help in risk identification and assessment. The art of the auditor is to uncover where material misstatements, fraud, or other issues are likely to exist. For example, AI tools can sift through historical data and detect trends associated with riskier transactions or business operations. AI can enhance the efficiency of the audit process by guiding auditors to unusual or potentially risky areas. The article, however, reveals that AI must be treated as an adjunct to an auditor and not as a substitute for the audit. Despite AI's capabilities, professional judgment is still necessary, as the results may require interpretation, verification, and context to understand.

One of the significant advantages of AI in auditing is its ability to enhance efficiency. AI can

Economics for Academic and Business. J. Safo execute repetitive tasks much more quickly than humans and can also work consistently on larger datasets. Information sorting, record comparison, extraction of relevant information, and anomaly detection can be automated and greatly expedited. This can help reduce the time auditors need to spend on routine tasks and allow them to focus on more advanced areas that require professional expertise. When used properly, AI can also boost productivity, reduce costs, and even enhance audit quality.

The article identifies key concerns about the complexity of AI systems, despite the benefits. Certain AI technologies are harder for users to understand, such as more sophisticated machine-learning systems. Sometimes an auditor may not be able to see that what enters the system is related to what leaves it. This poses an important problem, as the auditor should know and consider the evidence upon which they reach conclusions. An auditor may also find it hard to assess whether the output of an AI system is accurate, appropriate, and reliable if they cannot understand how the system arrived at the result.

Transparency is therefore very much related to auditability. An AI system could provide a correct answer, but an auditor must know the basis for that answer. For instance, if an AI tool flags a specific transaction as "high risk," the auditor should ideally be able to see this and investigate the reason for the decision. When transparency is inadequate, auditors may have difficulty verifying AI results or presenting findings to clients, regulators, and other stakeholders. This may raise issues of responsibility and accountability.

The issue of trust is also explored. If auditors are not familiar with the AI system, they will not fully trust the information it provides. Relying on AI should not be based solely on the assumption of the technology's accuracy. Rather, auditors require evidence of proper system design, testing, monitoring, and control. The trustworthiness of AI-generated outputs can be linked to the quality of the data used for training or for system use. The AI system can generate incorrect results if the input information is inaccurate, biased, or incomplete. As a result, auditors need to consider how AI can be used in the audit process, taking into account its capabilities and constraints.

Another major problem the article revealed is the lack of skills and knowledge among some auditors. As more businesses adopt AI, auditors need to acquire new skills and knowledge that go beyond accounting and auditing. There is a need for auditors to understand data analytics, machine learning, algorithmic decision-making, information systems, cybersecurity, and AI governance, among other areas. They do not have to be software developers, but they should have enough technical understanding to assess AI systems, challenge their results, and identify their vulnerabilities.

There are implications for education and professional development because the need for new skills is significant. Training programs for universities, professional accounting bodies, and employers may need to be adjusted to ensure that current and future auditors can collaborate effectively with AI. Conventional auditing training could be complemented with hands-on training in data analysis, digital technologies, and automated system assessment. AI technologies are rapidly advancing, and this will remain a key priority for continuous professional development.

The article thus brings up the opportunities and challenges of adopting AI in auditing. While AI has the potential to streamline, augment, and simplify the auditing process, it must be understood, controlled, and monitored to realise these benefits. The authors' focus on auditability leaves no doubt that

Economics for Academic and Business. J. Safo technological innovation should go hand in hand with transparency, accountability, human control, and adequate professional skills.

Evaluation Paragraph

In the context of my research, this article provides a detailed account of the advantages and disadvantages of using AI in auditing. This article is not about AI replacing the way auditors do their work, but how it can complement it, and the added responsibilities and risks AI places on auditors. The balanced view is significant in research on the evolving nature of auditors' work in a digital business world.

The topic of auditability is one of the best aspects of the article. The concept is fundamental, as it is not only the speed at which a system delivers results that defines its effectiveness in AI auditing. Auditors are expected to assess the reliability and appropriateness of those results, too. The article highlights a key concern that might be overlooked: ensuring that AI systems are transparent and comprehensible. While an AI system can be highly developed, it may be of little value in an audit if auditors cannot understand or validate its results.

Economics for Academic and Business. J. Safo

The article is also significant for its recognition of AI's potential to enhance the efficiency of auditing. Auditors handle a large volume of information, and it can be challenging and time-consuming to review all available data manually. AI offers ways to streamline repetitive tasks and process more data. This can aid auditors in detecting irregular activities and potential risks more effectively. The source thus corroborates the thesis that AI can enhance audit processes, provided it is used correctly and in conjunction with human intelligence.

One positive aspect is the article's consideration of the dangers of overreliance on AI. While AI can generate valuable insights, it does not necessarily provide accurate or unbiased data. The quality of its data, algorithms, and design is crucial for AI systems. The reliability of the outputs may be affected by data errors or system weaknesses. Thus, it underscores the need for human oversight, which the article highlights. While trusting AI-generated findings, auditors should also carefully verify them to ensure they have adequate supporting information to make professional judgments.

The article is also a valuable contribution for its discussion of the evolving skills auditors are required to possess. With the increasing prevalence of AI,

Economics for Academic and Business. J. Safo auditors must possess a blend of accounting and auditing understanding, along with technological skills. It reinforces the need to shift the focus from education and professional training to technological advances. All students entering the world of accounting and auditing should be familiar with digital technologies and data analytics to engage with AI-enabled tools confidently. Current professionals need ongoing training to ensure they remain up to date.

Another advantage is the focus on having the correct rules, controls, and governance. The adoption of AI in auditing cannot be done without addressing transparency and accountability, data quality, security, and human oversight. Establishing clear procedures can help organisations understand when to use AI, how to validate AI outputs, and who is responsible for any problems that arise. Good governance, in this regard, can help mitigate the risks of relying on AI inappropriately or too highly.

However, there are some constraints with the source. Its limitations are that it might not address every issue encountered when using AI in an easy-to-understand, user-friendly manner. The article highlights concerns about auditability, transparency, trust, and auditor competence, but readers may need to look elsewhere for practical ways organisations can overcome these issues. For instance, research could focus on specific AI auditing tools, training initiatives, governance structures, or organisational policies that have effectively increased AI adoption.

There is also the risk that some AI technologies and practices may evolve rapidly, so their suitability may need to be evaluated as they advance. AI systems are constantly evolving, and new tools are being released all the time. Hence, researchers must stay up to date with the latest research and expert advice to keep their knowledge of using AI in auditing current. However, its focus on principles such as transparency, auditability, professional judgment, and accountability remains applicable across different types of technology.

Overall, this article is a good and relevant source of information for research on artificial intelligence in auditing. It shows how AI has the potential to be highly beneficial, streamlining processes, handling large volumes of data, detecting risks, and assisting auditors with repetitive work. It also acknowledges challenges in transparency, trust, accountability, data quality, and professional competence in AI. The discussion in the article aligns with the notion that AI should be used responsibly, not just because of its technological sophistication.

The conclusion is that the future of auditing and inspection in this context is one in which more of the human and intelligent aspects will collaborate. AI can handle all the analysis and repetitive work, while auditors provide the contextualization, ethical judgement, and professional judgement. Auditors need to understand the systems they are auditing, and organisations need to establish appropriate controls and governance arrangements. The article is therefore helpful in that it does not eliminate human auditors, but offers the invaluable assistance of AI with the caution, clarity, and responsibility that is required. It is also clear from this that developing new technological skills is a unique focus of its work, and that education, as well as professional training, must adapt to meet the profession's changing needs.

Chapter 7
Major Factors That Businesses Should Consider When Expanding into International Markets

Major Factors That Businesses Should Consider When Expanding into International Markets

Introduction

International market expansion is an important growth strategy that enables businesses to access new customers, increase sales, diversify revenue sources, acquire resources, and strengthen their competitive position. Globalisation, technological development, digital trade, and improved transportation have made it easier for businesses to operate beyond their domestic markets. However, international expansion also exposes firms to political, economic, cultural, legal, financial, technological, and operational risks that may not exist or be less significant in their home countries. Therefore, international expansion should not be based solely on the attractiveness of a foreign market. Businesses need to conduct systematic market research and assess whether the target country offers suitable conditions for sustainable operations. The World Bank (2025) notes that businesses operating internationally continue to face challenges associated with geopolitical tensions, trade restrictions, inflation, policy uncertainty, and climate-related risks.

International expansion can take different forms, including exporting, licensing, franchising, strategic alliances, joint ventures, acquisitions, and wholly owned subsidiaries. The appropriate method depends on the company's resources, objectives, risk tolerance, industry characteristics, and conditions in the target market. Therefore, several major factors should be carefully considered before a business commits financial and human resources to international expansion.

Market Size and Market Potential

One of the most important considerations is the size and potential of the target market. Businesses should determine whether sufficient demand exists for their products or services. A large population does not automatically make a market attractive, as consumers may have low purchasing power, strong preferences for local products, or limited demand for the company's offerings. Companies should therefore examine population size, income levels, consumer spending, market growth, customer demographics, and future demand.

Market research should also identify whether the market is growing, stable, or declining. A growing market can provide opportunities for businesses to establish themselves before competition becomes intense. Businesses should analyse customer needs, purchasing behaviour, preferences, and unmet needs. They should also identify the size of the target customer segment rather than focusing only on the total population.

Digitalisation has further expanded international market opportunities, as companies can reach consumers without immediately establishing physical operations abroad. The WTO, IMF, OECD, and UNCTAD (2023) explain that digitally ordered and digitally delivered trade have become important components of international commerce. Consequently, businesses should assess both traditional and digital market opportunities when determining whether a country is attractive.

Economic Conditions

The economic environment of a foreign country significantly influences the success of an international expansion strategy. Businesses should examine gross domestic product (GDP), GDP growth, inflation, interest rates, unemployment, consumer income, exchange rates, and overall economic stability. A country experiencing strong economic growth may offer expanding consumer demand and increased business opportunities.

However, economic growth should be assessed together with purchasing power and income distribution. A country may have a large economy but still provide limited opportunities for a particular product if the target consumers cannot afford it. Businesses should therefore examine disposable income and purchasing power within their specific customer segments.

Exchange-rate conditions are particularly important because currency fluctuations can affect revenues, costs, profits, and the value of foreign investments. A company selling products in a foreign currency may experience lower profits if the foreign currency depreciates against its home currency. Similarly, importing raw materials may become more expensive when exchange rates move unfavourably. The World Bank (2025) identifies inflation, trade policy uncertainty, and geopolitical risks as continuing challenges for global economic activity.

Political Stability and Government Policies

Political stability is another major consideration. Businesses need to understand the political environment of the target country because changes in government, political conflict, corruption, civil unrest, or sudden policy changes can affect business operations. Governments may also introduce new taxes, investment restrictions, import controls, local ownership requirements, or industry regulations. Businesses should examine the government's attitude toward foreign investment and determine whether foreign companies receive equal treatment compared with domestic businesses. Countries with transparent institutions and predictable policies generally provide a more stable environment for long-term investment.

Geopolitical tensions have become particularly important for international businesses because they can affect investment decisions, supply chains, transportation, and market access. UNCTAD (2024) reports that geopolitical tensions, economic fragmentation, industrial policies, and supply-chain diversification have been reshaping international investment patterns. Therefore, businesses should conduct political risk assessments before entering foreign markets and develop contingency plans for potential disruptions.

Legal and Regulatory Environment

Businesses must understand the legal requirements of the country in which they intend to operate. Laws concerning company registration, employment, taxation, consumer protection, competition, intellectual property, data protection, environmental protection, imports, exports, and foreign ownership may differ substantially from those in the domestic market. Failure to comply with local laws can result in financial penalties, legal disputes, reputational damage, or withdrawal of operating licences. Businesses should therefore obtain appropriate legal advice and conduct regulatory due diligence before entering a foreign market.

Intellectual property protection is especially important for companies whose competitive advantage depends on brands, patents, software, designs, or proprietary technology. Businesses should determine whether the target country provides effective protection against counterfeiting, unauthorised use, and intellectual property theft.

Cultural Differences and Consumer Behaviour

Cultural differences can strongly influence international business performance. Products and marketing strategies that succeed in one country may fail in another because consumers may have different values, traditions, languages, beliefs, lifestyles, and purchasing habits. Businesses should therefore conduct cultural research before introducing products or promotional campaigns. Language is particularly important because direct translations may not convey the intended meaning and can sometimes lead to embarrassing or offensive interpretations. Advertising messages, packaging, colours, product names, and promotional techniques may all require adaptation. Consumer behaviour should also be examined. Customers in different countries may have different attitudes toward price, quality, convenience, customer service, status, sustainability, and brand loyalty. Successful international businesses therefore balance global consistency with local adaptation.

Competition and Industry Structure

Businesses should assess the competitive environment before entering a foreign market. This involves identifying existing competitors, their market shares, prices, product quality, distribution systems, customer loyalty, and competitive advantages. Local companies may possess significant advantages because they understand customer preferences, regulations, suppliers, and distribution channels. International firms may therefore need to offer a distinctive value proposition to compete effectively. This could involve lower prices, superior quality, innovative products, stronger customer service, technological advantages, or a well-established international brand.

Businesses should also consider the possibility of competition from other multinational corporations. Entering a market with numerous powerful competitors may require substantial investment in marketing and product development. A smaller or less competitive market may provide better opportunities, although businesses must ensure that demand is sufficiently strong.

Choice of Market Entry Strategy

Another major consideration is the method through which the business will enter the international market. Exporting is generally less expensive and less risky than establishing a wholly owned subsidiary because the company can test demand without making a large physical investment. However, exporting may provide less control over distribution and customer relationships. Licensing and franchising allow local companies to use the firm's brand,

Economics for Academic and Business. J. Safo technology, or business model in exchange for fees or royalties. These approaches can facilitate rapid international expansion while reducing investment requirements. However, businesses may have less control over quality and operations.

Joint ventures allow foreign and local companies to share resources, knowledge, risks, and ownership. They can be useful where local knowledge is essential or where regulations restrict foreign ownership. However, disagreements between partners can create significant management challenges. Wholly owned subsidiaries provide greater control but usually require greater financial commitment and expose the company to greater risk. Sudirjo (2023) suggests that research on international market entry emphasises that exporting, licensing, joint ventures, and wholly owned subsidiaries involve different levels of risk and control.

Financial Resources and Investment Requirements

International expansion requires adequate financial resources. Businesses should estimate the cost of market research, product adaptation, legal registration, facilities, employees, marketing, transportation, technology, taxes, insurance, and working capital. Companies should prepare detailed financial projections that include expected revenues, operating costs, break-even points, return on investment, and possible losses. They should also consider the cost of international money transfers and exchange rate fluctuations.

Financial planning is especially important for smaller businesses because international expansion can place considerable pressure on cash flow. A company may generate strong long-term opportunities but incur short-term losses as it establishes its brand and distribution network. UNCTAD (2025) indicates that international investment has been affected by geopolitical fragmentation, trade tensions, and uncertainty, underscoring the need for careful investment planning before committing substantial resources abroad.

Supply Chain and Infrastructure

Businesses must evaluate the quality and reliability of infrastructure in the target country. This includes roads, ports, airports, electricity, telecommunications, warehousing, internet connectivity, and logistics systems. Weak infrastructure can increase transportation costs, delay deliveries, reduce product quality, and negatively affect customer satisfaction. Supply-chain resilience is increasingly important because international businesses can be affected by wars, pandemics, natural disasters, trade restrictions, port disruptions, and raw material shortages. Companies should therefore avoid unnecessary dependence on a single supplier or transportation route.

UNCTAD (2024) observes that companies are increasingly diversifying supply chains in response to global economic and geopolitical changes. Businesses should consequently consider multiple suppliers, alternative transportation routes, local sourcing opportunities, and appropriate inventory levels.

Human Resources and Labour Conditions

Human resources are another essential consideration. Businesses need to determine whether the target market has sufficient skilled labour and whether employees possess the technical and managerial capabilities required by the business. Companies must also understand local employment laws concerning wages, working hours, benefits, recruitment, termination, health and safety, and employee rights. Cultural differences can influence leadership styles, communication, teamwork, motivation, and workplace relationships.

Businesses may need to employ local managers because they understand the language, culture, customers, regulations, and business environment. At the same time, expatriate employees may be needed to transfer organisational knowledge and maintain corporate standards. An effective balance between local and international employees can strengthen international operations.

Taxation and Trade Policies

Taxation can significantly influence the profitability of international operations. Businesses should examine corporate taxes, value-added taxes, customs duties, withholding taxes, import duties, and tax incentives offered to foreign investors. Trade agreements are also important. Regional and bilateral trade agreements may reduce tariffs and facilitate the movement of goods and services. Conversely, high tariffs, quotas, sanctions, and other trade restrictions may make a market less attractive.

The WTO (2023) emphasises the importance of rules-based international trade and cooperation in supporting more diversified and resilient international markets. Businesses should therefore investigate applicable trade agreements and restrictions before entering a new country.

Technology and Digital Capability

Technology has transformed international expansion by allowing businesses to reach customers through websites, social media, e-commerce platforms, mobile applications, and digital payment systems. Businesses should assess the level of digital infrastructure in the target country and determine whether consumers have access to reliable internet and digital payment services. Digital capability can reduce market-entry costs, particularly for service-based businesses. A company can sell software, consulting, education, financial services, or other digitally deliverable products internationally without establishing physical facilities.

The WTO (2025) reports that digitalisation can reduce trade costs, encourage online sales, increase productivity, and expand digitally delivered services. Therefore, businesses should consider digital channels as part of their internationalisation strategy rather than relying exclusively on physical stores and traditional distribution networks.

Social, Environmental, and Ethical Responsibilities

Businesses expanding internationally must also consider their social and environmental responsibilities. Consumers, governments, investors, and employees increasingly expect companies to operate responsibly. Businesses should assess issues such as labour rights, environmental pollution, climate risks, human rights, corruption, and responsible sourcing. Sheehy et al. (2023) recommend responsible business conduct across areas such as human rights, labour rights, environmental protection, bribery, consumer interests, taxation, technology, and supply chain due diligence. Companies that ignore these issues may experience reputational damage, regulatory problems, consumer boycotts, or difficulties attracting investment.

Environmental considerations are also becoming important because climate-related disasters can disrupt operations and supply chains. Businesses should therefore assess climate risks and consider sustainable production, energy efficiency, responsible sourcing, and waste reduction as part of their international strategy.

Risk Management and Contingency Planning

Finally, businesses should conduct comprehensive risk assessments before entering international markets. International businesses face political, economic, financial, legal, operational, technological, environmental, and reputational risks. Risk management should identify potential threats, estimate their likelihood and impact, and establish appropriate responses. Businesses can reduce risks through insurance, diversification, local partnerships, currency hedging, multiple suppliers, contractual protections, and contingency plans.

The current international investment environment demonstrates the importance of such planning. UNCTAD (2025) reports ongoing uncertainty stemming from geopolitical tensions, trade barriers, and changes in investment conditions. Businesses should therefore avoid assuming that current market conditions will remain unchanged.

Conclusion

In conclusion, international market expansion can provide businesses with significant opportunities for growth, diversification, innovation, and increased competitiveness, but it also introduces complex risks. Successful international expansion requires more than identifying countries with large populations or attractive markets. Businesses should evaluate market potential, economic conditions, political stability, legal requirements, cultural differences, competition, entry strategies, financial resources, infrastructure, human resources, taxation, technology, sustainability, and risk.

A systematic assessment of these factors enables businesses to select markets that match their capabilities and strategic objectives. The international environment is increasingly influenced by geopolitical tensions, digitalisation, supply chain disruptions, climate risks, and shifting trade policies. Consequently, businesses should adopt flexible strategies that allow them to respond to changing conditions. Ultimately, successful international expansion depends on combining detailed market research, appropriate entry strategies, strong financial planning, cultural understanding, regulatory compliance, effective risk management, and responsible business practices. Companies that carefully evaluate these factors are more likely to establish sustainable international operations and achieve long-term competitive advantage.

References

Development (UNCTAD). (2024). *World Investment Report 2024: Investment Facilitation and Digital Government*. Stylus Publishing, LLC.

Sheehy, B., Valderrama, N. B., & Villegas, M. (2023). OECD guidelines for multinational enterprises. In *Encyclopedia of Sustainable Management* (pp. 2488–2492). Cham: Springer International Publishing. https://link.springer.com/rwe/10.1007/978-3-031-25984-5_1182

Sudirjo, F. (2023). Marketing strategy in improving product competitiveness in the global market. *Journal of Contemporary Administration and Management (ADMAN)*, *1*(2), 63-69. https://www.neliti.com/publications/565714/marketing-strategy-in-improving-product-competitiveness-in-the-global-market

United Nations Conference on Trade & Development (UNCTAD). (2025). *World Investment Report 2025: International Investment in the Digital Economy.* Stylus Publishing, LLC.

World Bank Group. (2021). *Global Economic Prospects, January 2021*. World Bank Publications. https://doi.org/10.1596/978-1-4648-1612-3

World Trade Organisation. (2023). World Trade Report 2023: Re-globalisation for a secure, inclusive

Economics for Academic and Business. J. Safo
and sustainable future.
https://www.wto.org/english/res_e/publications_e/wtr23_e.htm

Author Qualifications

1. D.D, Doctor of Divinity
2. Certificate in Bible Studies
3. Theology
4. Laws
5. (LLM)Master of Laws.
6. Postgraduate Laws
7. Legal research
8. Business, CSR, Corporate social responsibility, and human Rights law.
9. Institutional development and management
10. International Law.
11. BA (Hons) Laws
12. Law: includes Criminal, Tort, Damages, Contract, Property, Equity and Trust, European Law, Public, Constitutional, Judicial Review, and Agency.
13. Advanced Dip. Business Law, Level 4: includes Employment, Agency, Damages, Tort, Contract, Employment Tribunal, etc.
14. Dip. Criminology
15. Accounting
16. BA (Hons)op.
17. Financial Accountant

Economics for Academic and Business. J. Safo

18. Management Accountant
19. Cert. Acct. (Certified Accountant)
20. (PCA) Professional Certificate in Financial and Management Accounting
21. Dip. Book-keeping, Level 3
22. Nursing
23. Nursing: RMN Registered Mental Nurse)
24. GN (General Trained Nurse)
25. Lecturer qualifications
26. DD Doctor of Divinity
27. LLM Master of Laws
28. BA (Hons)
29. BSc Hons o/g) Psychology with counselling
30. Cert. in Education (Lecturer)
31. Business Certificate in Advanced Management
32. Cert. Business Enterprise
33. Advanced Food Hygiene
34. Intermediate Health and Safety
35. Dip. Safety Management
36. International Entrepreneur for over 25 years
37. (NVQ); Internal Verifier (V1)
38. Trainer and Assessor A1 (NVQ)
39. Computers

Economics for Academic and Business. J. Safo

40. Diploma; Cisco Level 2 Technician (build, repair, networking)
41. Microsoft Specialist
42. Dip. Claire Plus (in all software)
43. New Clait Dip. Level 2
44. ECDL Level 2
45. Scriptwriter
46. Diploma in scriptwriting.
47. TV, radio, stage, and film
48. Diploma in writing
49. Autobiography
50. Biography
51. Family History
52. Certificate in Poetry
53. Psychology and Counselling
54. BSc (Hons o/g) Psychology with Counselling
55. Diploma in Counselling and Psychology
56. Cert. in Counselling and Psychology
57. Certificate in Social Science
58. Photography
59. Cert. (PGFP)
60. Portrait, Glamour and Figure
61. Plumbing
62. Level 3 City and Guilds
63. Hypnotherapy

64. Dip. Hypnotherapy

Author of over 202 book titles.

Faith Books

ALL Faith; Four Books in the English language

1. **Christianity;** Thirteen books in the English language
2. **Islam;** Four Books in the English language
3. **Buddhism;** One Book in the English language
4. **Hinduism;** Two Books in the English language
5. **Freemasonry**; One Book in the English language
6. **French Language;** Ten Books in Christianity/Islam/Hinduism/Theology.
7. **Spanish language;** Ten Books in Christianity/Islam/Hinduism/Theology.
8. **Arabic language;** Five Books in Christianity/Islam
9. **Chinese language;** Six Books in Christianity/Islam

Academic & Non-Faith Books

Economics for Academic and Business. J. Safo

10. **Laws**; Eleven Books for curious persons, six forms to master a master's degree, authored by a Master of Laws.
11. **Poems;** Thirteen Books covering every country in the world plus their capital city and map.
12. **Poems & Biography on religious figures;** One Book - Jesus Christ, Prophet Muhammad, Buddha, Guru, all major prophets, Archangels, Saints
13. **Ethics;** One Book - Covers all professions, religious faith and culture
14. **Accounts** / Finance; Five Books - Financial and management accounts.
15. **Automobile** / Engineering: Three Books - refers to the various advancements and innovations in vehicles
16. **Computer;** Seven Books - From inquisitive/beginners to advance/master's degree.
17. **Business;** Sixteen Books - All types; private, co-operate/institution; from set up/developing to management. Authored by experience and mastery.
18. **Agriculture**; Four Books - From beginners to advanced degree-level understanding of agriculture
19. **Women;** Four Books - All you need to know about women.
20. **Nursing/Medical / Health & Social Care;** Fifteen Books - From a curious person to a nursing degree

Economics for Academic and Business. J. Safo

21. Disorders & Mental Health; Three Books - From a curious person to a mental health degree
22. **Gynaecology & Midwifery** - Five Books - For a curious person to a nursing degree
23. **Philosophy:** Three Books - for a curious person to reach an undergraduate level.
24. **History/current affairs:** Nineteen Books - for a curious person to reach an undergraduate level.
25. **Geography:** Four Books - for a curious person to reach an undergraduate level.
26. **Biology:** Three Books - for a curious person to reach A level -SHS - Degree.
27. **Physics:** Three Books - for a curious person to reach A level -SHS - Degree.
28. **Chemistry**: Two Books - for a curious person to reach A level -SHS - Degree.
29. **Psychology: Seven Books - From a curious** person to undergraduate.
30. **Counselling: Five Books - From a** curious person to undergraduate.
31. **Social Science / Sociology & Education: Six Books** - From curious to undergraduate.
32. • **Mathematics:** Three Books - From a curious person to A level -SHS - Degree.
33. • **Research:** Two Books - from a curious person to A level - SHS - Degree.

34. • **Economics:** Two Books - for a curious person to A level - SHS - Degree.
35. **Sports:** One Book - for a curious person to A level - SHS - Degree.

ALL FAITHS

1. Theology
2. Love All Faiths
3. Faith Unity
4. Religion and Law; religion's influence on national and international laws.

CHRISTIANITY

1. Biblical Studies International AS & A Level
2. BIBLE New Testament; 1,111 QUESTIONS AND ANSWERS: Plus, synopsis and Test yourself
3. Bible Old Testament 1,064 Questions and Answers and synopsis
4. Jesus Christ is Coming Soon
5. God Loves Christianity
6. God's/Allah's Messengers
7. Islam v. Christianity
8. Jesus Christ is Coming Soon
9. Psychology of religion, politics, and marriage
10. Faith unity.
11. Faith unity: simplified version.
12. Islamism versus Christianity.
13. Love all faiths.

ISLAM (In English)

1. Islamic Studies
2. QUR'AN: 1,044 Questions & Answers.
3. Allah Loves Islam
4. Islam v. Christianity

BUDDHISM (In English)

1. God Enlighten Buddhism

HINDUISM (In English)

1. Hinduism Studies AS & A Level
2. Parama Nandra Loves Hindus

FREEMASON (In English)

1. In Search of Wisdom in Freemasonry

FRENCH BOOKS (Religious)

1. Théologie; 54 Essais. : Le chemin vers l'obtention du diplôme
2. CORAN; 1 044 questions et réponses. : Le chemin vers l'obtention du diplôme

3. BIBLE Nouveau Testament ; 1 111 Questions et Réponses: De plus, un résumé et testez-vous
4. Bible Ancien Testament : 1064 questions et réponses (French Edition)
5. Allah Aimel'islam (Allah loves Islam)

6. Aime toutes les fois (Love All Faiths)

7. Islamisme. V. christianisme (Islam v Christianity)

8. Dieu aime le christianisme (God loves Christianity)

9. Les Messagers De Dieu/Allah (God/Allah Messengers)

10. À la recherche de la sagesse dans la franc-maçonnerie (In Search of Wisdom)

SPANISH BOOKS (Religious)

1. CORÁN 1.044 preguntas y respuestas
2. BIBLIA Nuevo Testamento; : 1.111 PREGUNTAS Y RESPUESTAS
3. BIBLIA Antiguo Testamento: 1.064 preguntas y respuestas y sinopsis

4. Teología: 54 ensayos. : El camino hacia la graduación
5. En busca de la sabiduría masónica (In search of wisdom in Freemasonry)

6. Ametodas las creencias (Love All Faith)

7. Mensajeros de Dios (God Messengers)

8. Dios Ama El Cristianismo (God Loves Christianity)

9. Islam vs Cristianismo (Islam v Christianity)

10. Allah am el Islam (Allah Loves Islam)

ARABIC (Religious)

1. الله يحب الاسلام. (Allah loves Islam)

2. حب جميع الأديان Love All Faith

3. القرآن١٠٤٤ سؤال وجواب

4.1,06 سؤال وجواب وملخص: العهد القديم للكتاب المقدس

Economics for Academic and Business. J. Safo

5. علم اللاهوت: ٥٤ مقالة. الطريق إلى التخرج

CHINESE BOOKS (Religious)

Books in Chinese

1.伊斯蘭教訴基督教 (Islam v Christianity)

2. 上帝爱伊斯兰教 (Allah Loves Islam) - Traditional Chinese Edition

3. 圣经 新约

一千一百一十一 个问题与解答

另外，概要和测试自己

4. 圣经旧约

1,064 个问题与解答

以及剧情简介

5. 神学: 54 篇论文 毕业之路

6. 古兰经 (Quran): 1,044 个问题与解答

ACADEMIC AND NON-FAITH BOOKS- IN ENGLISH LANGUAGES

LAW

1. THE LAW: “AS” “A” Level/SHS: Cambridge
2. Global Injustice
3. The Journey to Law Graduation
4. THE JOURNEY TO MASTER OF LAWS
5. International Law plus 30 dissertation
6. Laws - United Kingdom +30 dissertation
7. The Law (Over 1,160 Questions and Answers)
8. Business Law volume 1; over 800 Q&A (contract, employment, types of HR
9. Business Law Volume 2: over 600 Q&A (Tort, CSR, Equity, Trust
10. Criminology: (Over 1,300 Questions and Answers)
11. Religion And Law

POEMS

1. 102 Poems on North America

2. 70 Poems on South American Countries and Cities
3. 80 Poems on the Arctic and Antarctica
4. 102 POEMS ON AUSTRALIA, OCEANIA, NEW ZEALAND
5. 101 Poems on Asian countries and cities
6. 118 USA POEMS: 50 States, Cities and Maps
7. 114 Poems on 54 African countries
8. Over 200 Love Poems plus over 100 love icebreakers
9. Over 100 Poems on Faith & Victory
10. 107 Poems on Discrimination, Racism & Suffering
11. Jesus Christ, Prophet, Archangels, Saint (Over 150 poems and Biography
12. The One - Over 130 Poems "DCF"
13. 105 Poems on 54 European countries & Cities

AGRICULTURE

1. The Beekeeper's Blueprint: Growing your apiary from the ground up
2. A Modern Approach to Agriculture
3. ADDING VALUE TO AGRICULTURE: Advanced level

Economics for Academic and Business. J. Safo

4. Roadmap to sustain agriculture in rural development

BUSINESS

1. Diploma in Business BTEC Level 3
2. Quantity Survey: Diploma in Technology
3. Building and Construction Management
4. Archives and Records Management
5. Additive Manufacturing: 3D
6. HOSPITALITY & TOURISM Travelling the world: Training guide
7. Project Management
8. Project Monitoring And Evaluation
9. Business AS and A level/SHS Cambridge award
10. Business AS and A level/SHS Pearson/Edexcel award
11. Developing and Managing Institutions and Organisations Volume 1
12. Developing and Managing Institutions and Organisations Volume 2
13. Set up and manage a business
14. How to set up a care home and care agency
15. How to manage a care Home and care agency

16. Care Home: Staff training

ETHICS

1. Ethics

COMPUTER

1. Computing for beginners+310 questions and answers.
2. How to Build and Upgrade a Computer and Network
3. The Path of Information to the Computer Screen
4. Computer Programming, Coding & Science Dissertation
5. Computer Science; Journey to Graduation: A/SHS- level
6. (ICT) Information and Communications Technology: Volume1, "A" Level/SHS Journey to Graduation
7. (ICT) Information and Communications Technology: Volume2, "A" Level/SHS Journey to Graduation

AUTOMOBILE / ENGINEERING

1. ENVIRONMENTAL MANAGEMENT

Economics for Academic and Business. J. Safo

2. CONSTRUCTION ENGINEERING AND MANAGEMENT: DISSERTATION PLUS 64 Q & A
3. Automobile Technology

ACCOUNTS / FINANCE

1. ACCOUNTING 100 Q & A with Marking Schemes: for International Students
2. Monetary policy
3. ACCOUNTING AS/A/SHS Level: 300 Revision Multiple Choice Questions
4. Financial Accounting (Over 1,241 Questions and Answers)
5. Management Accounting (1015 Questions & Answers Plus 100 Self-Assessment Questions)

PSYCHOLOGY

1. PSYCHOLOGY: A/SHS Level
2. Psychology: AS/SHS Level
3. Psychology: 850 Q & A Kindle Edition
4. Journey to Psychology Graduation Volume 1
5. Journey to Psychology Graduation Volume 2

Economics for Academic and Business. J. Safo

6. Psychology of Religion, Politics & Marriage
7. Psychology: Journey to Graduation, Volume 3: 35 Essays

COUNSELLING

1. Journey to Counselling Graduation Volume 1
2. Journey to Counselling Graduation Volume 2
3. Counselling: Journey to Graduation Volume 3
4. Counselling: Journey to Graduation Volume 4
5. Mood Disorder & Therapy

ACADEMIC AND NON-FAITH BOOKS CONTINUED - IN ENGLISH LANGUAGES

PHILOSOPHY

1. TIME SPENT IN COLLEGE AND PROTECTIVE FACTORS: Dissertation for the PhD in Philosophy
2. PHILOSOPHY 133 Q & A: Epistemology and Moral AS/A/SHS levels Volume 1
3. PHILOSOPHY 200 Q & A: Epistemology and Moral AS/A/SHS levels Volume 2

HISTORY

1. European History International A Level
2. Travel & Tourism Cambridge IGCSE
3. INJUSTICES IN SOUTHERN EUROPE 1945-2025
4. Injustices in Central and Eastern Europe 1945-2025
5. Injustice in Western and Northern Europe 1945-2025
6. INJUSTICES IN CENTRAL AND WEST ASIA: 1945-2025
7. INJUSTICES IN EAST & SOUTHEAST ASIA
8. INJUSTICES IN SOUTH AMERICA: 1945-2025
9. INJUSTICES IN NORTH AMERICA: 1945-2025
10. INJUSTICES IN AFRICA: 1945-2025
11. IGCSE HISTORY Q & A: Past Papers 2024 to 2025
12. IGCSE HISTORY Q & A: Past Papers 2023 to 2024
13. IGCSE HISTORY Q & A: Past Papers 2020 to 2022
14. Global Perspectives
15. History: AS/A/SHS Level
16. History: Journey to Graduation: 38 Essays
17. ENEMIES Within the Earth
18. Slavery And Suffering

Economics for Academic and Business. J. Safo

19. Slavery to Mastership

GEOGRAPHY

1. TECHNIQUES IN GEOGRAPHY
2. GEOGRAPHY of AFRICA
3. Physical Geography
4. Geography: The Road to Graduation: 30 Essays

1. **BIOLOGY**
   2. BIOLOGY; Journey to Graduation Volume 1: A Level/ SHS
   3. BIOLOGY; Journey to Graduation Volume 2: A Level/ SHS
   4. BIOLOGY; Journey to Graduation Volume 3 : A/SHS/Degree

PHYSICS

1. Psychology: 850 Q & A Kindle Edition
2. Physics; Journey to Graduation Volume 1: "A" Level/SHS
3. Physics: Journey to Graduation Volume 2: A level/ SHS
4. Physics; Journey to Graduation V3: "A" Level /SHS

CHEMISTRY

1. Chemistry: Journey to Graduation Volume 1: A level/ SHS/Degree
2. Chemistry: Journey to Graduation Volume 2: 33 Essays, A level/ SHS Paperback

Gynaecology & Midwifery

1. Obstetrics
2. GYNAECOLOGY: 411 Q&A
3. PREGNANCY DISEASES
4. Gynaecology
5. Midwifery

Medical/Nursing/ Health & Social

1. Nursing: Miscellaneous Topics: 15 Dissertations
2. DISEASES: Volume 2 plus Q & A
3. DISEASES: Volume 1 plus Q & A
4. RADIOLOGY: X-ray, MRI & CT scan
5. Drug Trafficking Trials in the UK: Drugs and Alcohol Abuse
6. Drug and Substance Abuse Rehabilitation
7. Health care: Training Guide; 24 Essays
8. Trauma: Emotional, physical and psychological
9. Community Health Nursing
10. Drugs for Diseases: 1,007 Questions and Answers

Economics for Academic and Business. J. Safo

11. Health and Social Care
12. Journey to Nursing Graduation: 51 Essays
13. Mental and Physical Diseases - Plus Nursing and 53 Dissertations
14. Health and Social Care Plus 50 Dissertations

Disorders & Mental Health

1. Mental Health in Africa
2. LANGUAGE AND SPEECH DISORDER
3. MENTAL HEALTH; Volume 1 : Plus 37 Q & A

Social Science & Education

1. Sociology; IGCSE Past Exam Papers
2. Q&A 2023 to 2025
3. Sociology IGCSE Past Exam Papers Q&A 2020 to 2022
4. EDUCATION: From Birth to Death
5. Sociology: AS/A/SHS Level
6. Understanding Sociology Science - Plus 56 Dissertations

WOMEN

1. Black Girls in School: Effect of Zero Tolerance
2. Love for Sale
3. Women are superior to men

Economics for Academic and Business. J. Safo

4. Sweet and Sour Women (plus over 500 love letters from women)

Mathematics

1. Mathematics; Journey to Graduation Volume 1: A level/ SHS
2. Mathematics; Journey to Graduation Volume 2: A level/ SHS
3. Mathematics; Journey to Graduation Volume 3: A level/ SHS

Research

1. EDUCATION RESEARCH: 10 DISSERTATIONS Volume 1
2. EDUCATION RESEARCH: 10 DISSERTATIONS Volume 2

Economic

1. ECONOMICS; "AS" & "A" Level/SHS: Road to Graduation. V.1
2. ECONOMICS; Road to Graduation. V2

Sports

1. SPORTS AND EXERCISE SCIENCE

2.

Glossary Economic

A

Alignment adjustment

The adjustment applied to the expenditure and income measures of Gross Domestic Product that allows ONS to balance these with the output measure of Gross Domestic Product.

Appreciation

An increase in the value of an asset or currency relative to another asset or currency.

Asset

An item or claim that usually provides a flow of benefits – either income or services – to its owner. Real assets include land, buildings or machinery owned. Financial assets include cash and securities, and credit extended to customers.

B

B - Balance of payments

The accounting record of UK transactions with the rest of the world, including international institutions. Also known as the Pink Book.

Balance sheet

A statement, drawn up at a particular point in time, recording the assets held by and financial claims (liabilities) of a business, organisation or country.

Base rate

Set by the Bank of England in the conduct of monetary policy, it is the interest rate that commercial banks use as the basis for their lending rates to the public.

Basic prices

Prices excluding taxes and subsidies on products.

Blue Book

The familiar name of the 'United Kingdom National Accounts' produced annually by ONS. It contains estimates of Gross Domestic Product measured by the output, expenditure and income approaches.

Bond

A financial instrument that usually pays interest to the holder, issued by governments, companies and other institutions. Most bonds have a fixed date on which the borrower will repay the holder.

Business cycle

The short-run fluctuations of output around its long-term trend.

C

C - Capital

One of the factors of production, providing a stream of revenues or services to its owner. Capital can include tangible assets – such as plant or machinery – or intangible assets – such as software and knowledge.

Central Bank

The national institution that oversees the monetary system, ensures the health of the financial system and acts as lender of last resort.

Chained Volume Measures (CVM)

These time series have the effects of inflation removed by considering changes in quantity between consecutive periods, holding prices from previous periods constant.

Claimant count

The total number of individuals claiming Job Seekers Allowance (JSA).

Compensation of employees

Total remuneration payable to employees in cash or in kind, including the value of social contributions payable by the employer.

Constant Price (KP) series

These series have the effects of inflation removed by holding prices at the level of a chosen base year throughout the series (also known as “real terms” series).

Consumer prices

Prices offered to the public at the point of sale.

Consumer Price Index (CPI)

A measure of the price level in the economy based on the prices of a collection of goods that are designed to reflect the consumption basket of the average consumer.

Consumption

Expenditure on goods and services designed to satisfy individual or collective wants, as distinct from their purchase for use in business processes.

Contagion

The transmission of an economic shock in one economy to other nearby or linked economies.

Cost-benefit analysis

The identification, measurement and comparison of the costs and benefits associated with a specific project or intervention to determine its net value.

Current account

Details the UK's trade in goods and services with the rest of the world, as well as current transfers and income flows into and out of the UK from cross-border investments.

Current price (CP) series

These series include the effects of inflation.

D

D - Debt

An obligation or liability to make a payment or a payment in kind.

Deficit

Occurs when outward financial flows exceed inward financial flows. A “government deficit” occurs when expenditure exceeds the value of tax revenues and asset sales in a given period.

Deflation

A decline in the general price level in an economy, signified by an annual inflation rate below 0% (negative).

Deflator (implied)

A series that shows price changes and can be used to convert nominal values into “real” values, which are adjusted for the effects of inflation. An implied deflator is a series that shows the implied change in average prices for a variable by dividing the current price series by the real or volume series.

Depreciation

A fall in the value of an asset or currency relative to another asset or currency.

Direct taxation

Taxes on income, profits and wealth, paid directly by the bearer to the tax authorities.

Disposable income

Household income after the deduction of taxes and the addition of benefits.

Dividend

A payment made to company shareholders from current or previously retained profits.

E

E - Economics

The study of the allocation of scarce resources to satisfy individual and collective wants.

Euro area

The group of European countries that have officially adopted the euro (€) as their currency.

European Central Bank (ECB)

The central bank for the economies that are using the Euro currency, responsible for conducting monetary policy in the euro area.

European System of Accounts (ESA)

An integrated system of economic accounts. The United Kingdom National Accounts have been based on ESA 1995 since September 1998.

Exchange rate

The value of one currency in terms of a second currency.

Exports

Goods or services sold to agents in other countries; the opposite of imports.

F

Factory gate prices

Also known as output prices, these are the prices at which UK manufacturers sell goods. They include costs such as labour, raw materials, and energy, as well as interest on loans, site maintenance, or rent.

Final consumption expenditure

The expenditure on those goods and services used for the direct satisfaction of individual or collective needs, as distinct from their purchase for use in business processes.

Financial Intermediation Services Indirectly Measured (FISIM)

This represents the implicit charge for the service provided by monetary financial institutions, paid for by the interest differential between borrowing and lending rather than through fees and commissions.

Fiscal policy

Taxation and spending measures that allow the government to guide the economy.

Foreign Direct Investment (FDI)

Investment by firms in another country. Outward FDI is investment by UK-based firms in overseas markets. Inward FDI is investment by overseas firms in the UK. This is usually achieved through the acquisition of another firm or the establishment of new operations.

Frictional unemployment

The number of people who are classed as unemployed while they are moving between jobs.

Full employment

A state of the labour market in which everyone willing and able to work at the current wage rate is in employment, excluding those who are frictionally unemployed.

G

G – GDP(O), GDP(E), GDP(I)

These are 3 methods for calculating gross domestic product (GDP), a measure of economic activity. In theory, these 3 measures should be equal. GDP(O) is the sum of all production activity in the economy (the output approach), as estimated using gross value added (GVA). GDP(E) is the sum of all final expenditures by the economy (the expenditure approach). GDP(I) is the sum of all income generated by production within the economy (the income approach).

Gilt-edged securities (shortened to gilts)

Bonds issued by the UK government. These assets usually offer a low but certain return. Gilts are equivalent to US Treasuries and German Bunds.

Government debt

The accumulated borrowing of central and local government.

Government expenditure

Spending by national and local government and some government-backed institutions.

Government revenue

The money government receives from taxation, plus non-tax revenues such as money from government-owned firms.

Gross Capital Formation (GCF)

The sum of the value of gross fixed capital formation, changes in inventories and acquisitions less disposals of valuables for a unit or sector.

Gross Domestic Product (GDP)

A measure of the economic activity produced by a country or region.

Gross Fixed Capital Formation (GFCF)

Acquisitions less disposals of fixed assets and improvements to land.

Gross National Product (GNP)

GDP plus net income from abroad.

Gross Value Added (GVA)

The value generated by any unit engaged in production and the contributions of individual sectors or industries to Gross Domestic Product.

H

Human Development Index (HDI)

A composite statistic based on healthcare, education and economic statistics designed to rank countries by their level of development.

Hyper-inflation

A period of very high rates of inflation, usually leading to a loss of confidence in an economy's currency.

I

Imports

Purchases of foreign goods and services; the opposite of exports.

Income tax

A tax on earnings.

Index numbers

Data relative to a given base value, which typically refers to a year.

Indirect taxation

Taxes on expenditure (e.g. VAT). They are paid to the tax authorities, not by the consumer, but indirectly by the suppliers of the goods or services.

Inflation rate

The annual rate of change of the average price of goods and services.

Intangible assets

Intangible fixed assets include mineral exploration, computer software and entertainment, and literary and artistic originals. Expenditure on them is part of gross fixed capital formation. They exclude non-produced intangible assets such as patents, leases, transferable contracts, and purchased goodwill, the expenditure on which would be intermediate consumption.

Interest rate

The cost of borrowing expressed at an annual rate: the amount of interest that would be paid during a year divided by the amount of money loaned.

Intermediate consumption

The consumption of goods and services in the production process. It may be contrasted with final consumption and capital formation.

International Monetary Fund (IMF)

A Fund set up as a result of the Bretton Woods Conference of 1944 and that began operations in 1947. It includes most of the world's major economies. The Fund was set up to supervise the fixed exchange rate system agreed at Bretton Woods and to make available to its members a pool of foreign exchange resources to assist them when they have balance-of-payments difficulties.

Inventories (also known as stocks)

Consist of finished goods (held by the producer before sale, further processing or other use) and products (materials and fuel) acquired from other producers to be used for intermediate consumption or resold without further processing.

Investment

Spending on capital goods.

L

Liabilities

A claim on an institutional unit by another body that gives rise to a payment or other transaction transferring assets to the other body.

Liquidity

The ease with which a financial instrument can be exchanged for goods and services. Cash is very liquid whereas a life assurance policy is less so.

M

Macroeconomics

The branch of economics that deals with the whole economy in terms of aggregated variables such as output, consumption, investment, government spending and net trade.

Manufacturing

As a general rule, activities in the manufacturing section involve transforming materials into new products. Their output is a new product.

Market failure

Instances in which a market outcome results in a suboptimal or inefficient allocation of resources. These include situations of imperfect information, barriers to entry or natural monopoly.

Microeconomics

The branch of economics that studies individual economic agents and units: individuals, households, firms and industries.

Mixed income

The balancing item in the income account for household-owned unincorporated businesses. The owner or members of the same household often provide unpaid labour inputs to the business. The surplus is therefore a mixture of remuneration for such labour and return to the owner as entrepreneur.

Monetary policy

Policy to affect the supply or cost of money (rate of interest).

Money supply

The amount of money available in an economy.

Multi-factor productivity (MFP)

The difference between the rate of change of output and the rate of change of total inputs. It is calculated as a residual, which can be thought of as capturing technological progress, including the effect of changes in management techniques and business processes or more efficient use of factor inputs.

Multiplier effect

A measure of how one economic action influences other economic activities. The fiscal multiplier, for instance, is the amount that GDP increases for each extra pound of expenditure. For example, government spending on a new hospital could also see businesses benefit that supply the hospital and local retail outlets for the staff.

N

National accounts

An integrated description of all economic activity within the economic territory of the UK, including activity involving both domestic units (i.e. individuals and institutions resident in the UK) and external units (those resident in other countries).

National debt

The accumulated effect of budget deficits (less surpluses): the total stock of outstanding government debt.

National income

Everything produced, earned and spent in a country. An economy's net national product, subtracting depreciation from GNP at basic prices.

Natural rate of unemployment

The lowest rate of unemployment at which job markets can be in stable equilibrium.

Non-profit institutions serving households (NPISH)

An institutional sector consisting of non-profit institutions that are not mainly financed and controlled by government and provide goods or services to households for free or at prices that are not economically significant. These include bodies such as charities, universities, churches and trade unions.

Non-seasonally adjusted

A series that includes seasonal or calendar effects.

O

Office for Budget Responsibility (OBR)

Created in 2010 to produce official independent forecasts of the UK economy as well as authoritative analysis of the UK's public finances.

Opportunity cost of a good

The quantity of other goods sacrificed to get another unit of that good.

Output gap

The difference between actual and potential output.

P

Potential output

Output when all inputs are fully employed.

Producer prices

The prices faced by producers. The input price is the cost of goods bought by UK manufacturers for use in manufacturing. The output price (factory gate price) is the price at which UK manufacturers sell goods.

Productivity

A measure of the efficiency of output relative to inputs. For example, productivity will have increased if more is produced with the same number of inputs. It can be applied to the individual factors of production – most commonly labour – or collectively.

Purchasing Power Parity (PPP)

The path of the nominal exchange rate that would maintain a constant real exchange rate. Nominal exchange rate changes offset inflation differentials between countries.

Q

Quantitative Easing (QE)

A form of monetary policy in which a Central Bank buys financial assets – usually government bonds – to raise the money supply in an economy.

Quarterly National Accounts (QNA)

The third estimate of UK GDP based on around 92% of all survey data.

R

Real exchange rate

A country's exchange rate adjusted for the relative price movements of tradable goods and services.

Real household disposable income

The amount of income available for a household after taxes and subsidies, adjusted to remove the effects of inflation.

Real interest rate

The real rate of return on an asset, calculated by adjusting the interest received by the rate of inflation.

Retail prices

The price of goods offered to the consumer.

RPI, RPI(X), RPI(Y), RPI(J)

The Retail Prices Index (RPI) is a measure of inflation, but unlike the CPI, it incorporates housing costs. RPI(X) excludes mortgage interest payments; RPI(Y) is adjusted for changes in interest rates and indirect taxes; and RPI(J) uses an alternative calculation method for some prices that aligns with international standards. The RPI is not a National Statistic.

S

Saving ratio

The ratio of personal saving to disposable income.

Seasonally adjusted

A widely used technique for removing seasonal or calendar effects from time series data.

Services

A large and diverse grouping of industries that produce intangible economic output.

Services Producer Prices Index (SPPI)

Contains individual price indices that provide information on price change for a limited range of service industries.

Standard Industrial Classification (SIC)

The industrial classification applied to the collection and publication of a wide range of economic statistics.

Structural unemployment

Reflects a mismatch between skills and job opportunities as the pattern of demand and supply shifts.

U

ILO unemployment

The International Labour Organisation's measure of unemployment is defined as a person who is either out of work and actively seeking a job or out of work and waiting to start a job within the next two weeks.

Unit labour costs

Reflect total labour costs, including social security and employers' pension contributions, and including the costs of self-employed labour, incurred in the production of a unit of economic output.

V

Value Added Tax (VAT)

A consumption tax, which is paid to the tax authorities by the seller on behalf of the consumer. It is not levied on goods used as intermediate consumption.

www.ingramcontent.com/pod-product-compliance
Lightning Source LLC
LaVergne TN
LVHW050814061126
851857LV00012B/793
* 9 7 8 1 9 1 7 7 5 3 5 4 8 *